HOCKEY
IN
CLEVELAND

Richfield Coliseum in Summit County would play host to Cleveland hockey's Barons, Crusaders, and Lumberjacks before the end of its glory days. The Coliseum would also be used for everything from NBA games and boxing matches to concerts. During its 20-year run, many of the top names in sports and music from Larry Bird to Stevie Wonder would pass through the doors of this once spectacular venue. (Photograph courtesy Cleveland Press Collection/CSU Archives.)

FRONT COVER: Right wing Al MacAdam (foreground) and center Dennis Maruk were the leading scorers and two bright spots in the otherwise bleak existence of the National Hockey League's Cleveland Barons. The NHL only lasted two seasons in Cleveland as the Barons were hampered by losses and financial difficulties. The Barons, the last major American sports franchise to cease operations, merged with the Minnesota North Stars in 1978. (Photograph courtesy Cleveland Press Collection/CSU Archives.)

COVER BACKGROUND: This was the view from the loge level during a January 1978 Cleveland Barons game against the Buffalo Sabres. The Barons only lasted two season in the National Hockey League. (Photograph courtesy Cleveland Press Collection/CSU Archives.)

BACK COVER: Skating out of their signature "monster head," the Lake Erie Monsters took the ice in 2007 to start the latest chapter of professional hockey history in Cleveland. (Courtesy of the Lake Erie Monsters.)

HOCKEY
IN
CLEVELAND

Jon Sladek

ARCADIA
PUBLISHING

Published by Arcadia Publishing
Charleston, South Carolina

Library of Congress Control Number: 2013934878

For all general information, please contact Arcadia Publishing:
Telephone 843-853-2070
Fax 843-853-0044
E-mail sales@arcadiapublishing.com
For customer service and orders:
Toll-Free 1-888-313-2665

Visit us on the Internet at www.arcadiapublishing.com

Dedicated to Joel.

CONTENTS

FOREWORD

The Cleveland Barons will always be in my heart because it was one of my first opportunities to play in the greatest professional hockey league in the world. Along with most of the other players, I lived in the northwestern part of Akron. We played in the new Richfield Coliseum, which was a nice big arena southeast of Cleveland, not far from Akron.

The unfortunate part was that we did not get too many people out for the games. It was difficult to play knowing the team was going through financial struggles. If the NHL Players' Association had not stepped in, the team would have folded midway through the season and all of us players would have gone into a draft. This was tough as a player because you wanted to play for yourself instead of the team in the hopes of getting picked up by another NHL team.

I really enjoyed team owners George and Gordon Gund, who really liked hockey. I guess when you do not get a lot of fan support, the owners need to look at better situations. I still wonder if the NHL really gave the city of Cleveland enough time to establish a good fan base. We had some really good hockey players on those Barons teams, including wingers J.P. Parise, Al MacAdam, and Bob Murdoch; defensemen Bob Stewart and Jean Potvin; center Ralph Klassen; and goalie Gilles Meloche. The famous "3M Line" of Maruk, MacAdam, and Murdoch would have made the fans of Ohio extremely proud if we would have had more years to play there together.

Although it was only a couple years in Cleveland, I will always remember the great fan support for me.

—Dennis Maruk, Cleveland Barons 1976–1978

ACKNOWLEDGMENTS

First and foremost, thanks to my amazing wife/research assistant/copy editor Kourtney, who just knows how to get things done. She can now add "Cleveland hockey historian" to her resume.

I would like to thank the wonderful people who helped me acquire images: the Cleveland State University archives, the Lake Erie Monsters organization, Ashley Miller from Landov Media, and Jay Sharp from Sharp Imaging.

Special thanks to the Fritsche family for your cooperation. Also, to everyone at Arcadia Publishing for the great work you do.

Thanks to my mom, Robin, and stepdad, Don Natterer, for encouraging me to pursue dreams and to my dad, Dave Sladek, for getting me into sports. Also, to Brian "Shnydes" Snyder for consistent encouragement.

Thanks to Mark Price, Eric Metcalf, and the 1990s Cleveland Indians for making my youth more enjoyable. Most importantly, thanks to my Lord and savior Jesus, who makes everything possible.

Unless otherwise noted, all images appear courtesy of Cleveland State University, Cleveland Press Collection.

INTRODUCTION

The fans kept streaming through the gates. In all, 18,626 of them packed the Quicken Loans Arena for a hockey game between the Lake Erie Monsters and Texas Stars on January 22, 2010. The group of spectators was one of the largest in the long history of the American Hockey League. The crowd was nine times the capacity of the first arena that housed professional hockey in Cleveland. It was a testament to how far the sport had come since its humble beginnings a century ago.

If you have ever enjoyed a famous popcorn ball from the Humphrey Company, a Cleveland staple for generations, then you are connected to the origins of pro hockey in northeast Ohio. Most known for their popcorn and ownership of Euclid Beach amusement park, the Humphrey family provided the conduit through which Canada's top sport arrived on the southern shore of Lake Erie.

The Humphreys sought to build a family entertainment venue for the winter months when their wildly popular Euclid Beach Park was closed. In doing so, they inadvertently helped bring hockey to Cleveland. In 1907, the Elysium ice arena was built at the corner of East 107th and Euclid Avenue. The facility not only provided a large ice surface, but also enough seating for more than 2,000.

Soon, amateur hockey leagues began playing at the Elysium as the sport rapidly grew in popularity. After a couple decades of amateur play, a former National Hockey League goaltender named Harry Holmes took notice. The Canadian native viewed Cleveland as an untapped hockey market and prime location to move his International Hockey League team. After forging an agreement with the Humphrey family to play at the Elysium, Holmes officially brought the first professional hockey team to Cleveland. They were named the "Cleveland Indians" after the famous baseball team in town. The hockey Indians officially opened on November 16, 1929, and the first season was all joy for the team and its fans. They finished atop the eight-team league with a 24-9-9 record and won the IHL title.

The stock market crash of 1929 and the Great Depression took a profound toll on the country. Harry Holmes's Indians were not exempt. As crowds dwindled when people could no longer afford luxuries like attending sporting events, Holmes struggled to put adequate teams on the ice. The Indians plummeted in the standings, which led to even worse attendance.

After Cleveland's third straight last-place finish in 1934, Holmes was desperate for a buyer for his squad, and in stepped a savior, Al Sutphin. A prominent local businessman, Sutphin purchased the Cleveland hockey club and immediately changed the name to the Cleveland Falcons. While Sutphin's Falcons played three unremarkable seasons from 1934–1937, the visionary's big impact came off the ice. Carrying out a seemingly unattainable dream, Sutphin privately financed a new, state-of-the-art, 10,000-seat arena for his team. As the facility was constructed, Clevelanders were shocked such a building could be erected at the height of the Great Depression. Sutphin's new arena would cement the city of Cleveland as a legitimate professional hockey town.

In 1937, the Cleveland Arena was the catalyst that launched what was to become the golden age of hockey in northeast Ohio. The Falcons were renamed "The Barons" and embarked on a nearly four-decade run of success that would never be matched in the American Hockey League.

A DYNASTY IS BORN

When Al Sutphin's Barons began playing in the Cleveland Arena in 1937, the climate was perfect for such a franchise to take the city by storm. With just six teams playing in the NHL, there existed a large pool of talented hockey players available for the taking. Also, with the Barons not restricted by an NHL affiliation, they were free to pursue any player of their liking.

The divide between the NHL and AHL was not what it is today. Top-tier players could earn as much money playing for the Barons in Cleveland as they would with one of the NHL teams. Also, few cities in the country had a facility as large and spectacular as the Arena.

The Barons responded, in just their second season, by winning the AHL's top prize, the Calder Cup, after an unimpressive 23-22-9 regular season record. Clevelanders began to routinely fill the downtown ice house to watch the hometown squad. During the 1940–1941 season, the Barons outdrew half the NHL teams, averaging 8,267 fans per contest. That season culminated in another championship.

Not surprisingly, with the Barons enjoying great success on the ice and at the gate, the NHL came knocking on Cleveland's door in 1942. Sutphin's decision, which should have been a no-brainer, was complicated by World War II. Both professional hockey leagues were feeling the effects of the war's extensive impact on the nation.

Sutphin, being a man of character, made a decision that altered the course of pro hockey in Cleveland forever. With the Barons still drawing well at home and on the road, he knew a jump to the big leagues would all but doom the AHL. Having already lost a couple teams, the league's main attraction fleeing would be a most devastating blow. For this reason, Al Sutphin declined the NHL invitation.

The rejection was not received well by the NHL, but the effects would not be felt until years later. The Barons continued to flourish for the rest of the decade. They captured another Calder Cup in 1945, once again besting Hershey in the final series. During the 1945–1946 season, the average attendance (10,146) actually eclipsed the building's capacity (9,847). The team fell just short of another title that year, losing the Calder Cup finals by one game to the Buffalo Bisons.

Two years later, the Barons would get revenge on those Bisons, sweeping them in the finals for Cleveland's fourth Calder Cup in 10 seasons. That Barons team finished the season at 43-13-12 after an unbelievable 27-game unbeaten streak. With the team riding high, Sutphin stunned the region by selling the franchise to businessmen from Minneapolis in 1949. Al Sutphin turned his 1934 investment of $1,700 into a $2 million payoff 15 years later.

The dynasty Sutphin built did not miss a beat after his departure. Cleveland captured a fifth Calder Cup in 1951, led largely in part by future hall-of-fame goalie Johnny Bower. The following spring, 10 years after declining the NHL's invitation, the Barons applied for entry into the big leagues. Even though they complied with all the NHL's prerequisites, the Barons were ultimately denied by a vote on July 2, 1952.

The official reason given by the NHL was "financial concerns." However, other theories existed. Some felt this was the big league's way of exacting revenge on the Cleveland franchise for 1942. Others felt Detroit Red Wings owner James Norris was behind the rejection. With just six teams in the NHL, Norris had significant control over three of them. In addition to owning the Wings, he owned the facility that housed the Chicago Blackhawks, as well as the real estate where the New York Rangers played.

Predictably, the Toronto Maple Leafs, Boston Bruins, and Montreal Canadiens voted in favor of admitting the Barons, while Detroit, Chicago, and New York opposed. Once again, the disappointment failed to translate onto the ice. The Barons continued to dominate, winning back-to-back Calder Cups in 1953 and 1954, giving the franchise seven total championships. Amazingly, they added an eighth in 1957 after losing in the finals the previous year. With four titles in the decade, there was no disputing who the team of the 1950s was.

The continued excellence of the Barons in the 1950s can be attributed mostly to Fred Glover. Arriving in 1953, Glover would play in 992 games for Cleveland through 1968, putting together arguably the greatest career in AHL history. When he retired, Glover was the league's all-time leader in goals, assists, and points. To this day, he remains second in each category.

Glover assumed the role of player/coach in 1962 and guided the team to an improbable postseason run two seasons later. After finishing the 1963–1964 season at just 37-30-5, the Barons caught fire in the playoffs. In the finals, the Barons swept the Quebec Aces in four straight games to take home an unprecedented ninth Calder Cup.

The euphoria of the championship in 1964 would be short lived. The hockey world was rapidly changing. The NHL was planning an expansion and AHL teams took on a greater role of feeder system as affiliation agreements were forged. Cleveland could no longer operate independently and buy superior players by matching NHL salaries. Fan interest also began to wane. With the arena nearly 30 years old and the team not winning as consistently, capacity crowds were no longer commonplace. When the Barons collapsed to 24-43-5 in the 1964–1965 season, attendance dipped to 3,722 a game. The glory days were officially over.

Sweeping changes came about in 1968. First was the departure of the legendary Fred Glover. The three-time AHL Most Valuable Player, now 40 years old, decided to hang up the skates and pursue a full-time coaching job in the NHL. Next was another change in ownership. This time the buyer was Cleveland attorney Nick Mileti.

For the same price Al Sutphin received for the Barons in 1949, Mileti purchased the franchise and the Cleveland Arena. While Mileti hoped to revitalize the organization, his ultimate goal was to finally get the Barons into the NHL. Initially, the ambitious owner would fail on both fronts. Average attendance plummeted to a sad 3,415 for the season. Also, the NHL again snubbed northeast Ohio, this time due to the aging Cleveland Arena, which was now deemed too small to house a major league hockey team.

When the World Hockey Association formed to compete with the NHL, Mileti jumped at the opportunity. The minute he was approved for a WHA franchise was the minute the original Barons died. The 1972–1973 season began with both teams competing for fan interest and the Barons getting clobbered. The team that once averaged more than 10,000 a game now struggled to top 1,000.

Nick Mileti mercifully pulled the plug on the franchise and sold it to a group in Jacksonville, Florida, midway through the season. Just 435 fans bothered to show up for the Barons' final game in Cleveland on February 4, 1973. It was a sad end to one of the greatest franchises in the history of the American Hockey League.

Shown is an inside view of the Elysium located at East 107th and Euclid Avenue. The Humphrey family, known for its popcorn company and Euclid Beach amusement park, built the facility in 1907 to give the community an alternative family entertainment venue during the cold winter months when Euclid Beach was closed. The Elysium also hosted traveling ice shows and provided free skate sessions or professional skating lessons. Almost immediately, local hockey enthusiasts began organizing amateur leagues and the sport rapidly expanded in popularity.

Pictured above is construction on the Elysium in 1907; below is an exterior view of the finished product. As amateur play flourished at the arena, it caught the attention of former Canadian hockey pro Harry "Hap" Holmes. While the seating capacity was only around 2,000, few cities in the country had such a facility. Holmes ultimately brought the first professional hockey team to Cleveland to play in the Elysium in 1929. Within a decade, the sport had outgrown the building.

A DYNASTY IS BORN

Above is a street view of the Cleveland Arena at 3717 Euclid Avenue, financed by Barons owner Al Sutphin. One of the premier pro hockey facilities when it was built in 1937, the arena housed the original American Hockey League Barons for their entire existence. It was also home to the World Hockey Association's Cleveland Crusaders and the National Basketball Association's Cavaliers. Clevelanders routinely filled the building to capacity during the Barons' glory years. As seen at right, what was a premier sports palace in the late 1930s was an aging, dilapidated relic in the 1970s.

These programs are from the Cleveland Arena. There was no better place to be in the mid-20th century than the arena. In addition to hockey, the building hosted what is widely considered the first rock and roll concert ever, the Moondog Coronation Ball in 1952. The arena also hosted the Cincinnati Royals of the National Basketball Association, which led to Cleveland getting its own team a few years later.

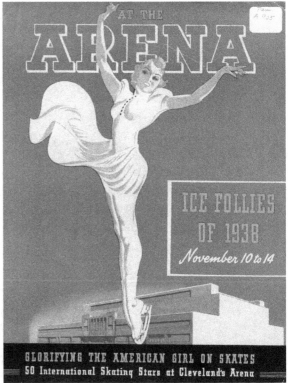

The 1952–1953 Barons pose with the Calder Cup, the American Hockey League's championship trophy. After a dominant 42-20-2 regular season, Cleveland outlasted a stingy Pittsburgh Hornets team four games to three in the finals to capture a sixth title for the city. The Barons added another the following season.

The Cleveland Falcons are in action against the Buffalo Bisons in a 1934 game at the Elysium. When Al Sutphin purchased the future Barons, he immediately knew the team would soon outgrow the 2,000-seat converted skating rink. Three years later, the team had a new name, uniforms, and state-of-the-art facility to play in.

Here, the Cleveland Falcons show off their new purple and white uniforms featuring an orange falcon as they skate toward the goal in this 1937 matchup. The team would last just one season.

A DYNASTY IS BORN

Young amateurs Hal Dewey (left), Norm Burns (middle), and Gerry Brown, in Cleveland to train, look longingly at a Barons jersey they hope to wear. Only Burns would ever play for the Barons, spending part of the 1946–1947 season in Cleveland. Brown would enjoy the most successful career, playing nine American Hockey League seasons and two stints with the Detroit Red Wings.

Johnny Bower (left), seen here in 1949, was the best goaltender to play for the Barons. Nicknamed "the China Wall," Bower spent nine seasons and won three Calder Cups in Cleveland. Bower went on to lead NHL teams to four Stanley Cups and was inducted into the Hockey Hall of Fame in 1976. Al Rollins (right) spent just six games with the Barons before embarking on a lengthy major league career.

Defenseman Jim "Bulldog" Drummond (left) spent just one season in Cleveland after appearing in two games with the New York Rangers. Center Jack "Rabbit" Lavoie was a little man who came up big during the 1948 title run. Lavoie contributed eight points in nine games as the Barons earned another trophy.

With America and Canada both gearing up to join World War II and many men leaving for service, hockey teams were left looking for new talent quickly. Amateur clubs like Quebec's Senior Hockey League were a good place to start. Pictured are brothers Tony and Albert Lemay of the Ottawa Commandos. (QSHL.)

A DYNASTY IS BORN

Hershey defenseman and future National Hockey League mainstay Claire Martin crushes Cleveland's Ken Schultz in a 1949 game. This picture is indicative of the rivalry the Bears and Barons shared as the American Hockey League's elite teams. To date, no team has won more Calder Cups than either the Bears or the Barons.

Walter "Babe" Pratt (left) and goalie Roger Bessette are seen here during the magical 1947–1948 championship season. Pratt would be traded to Hershey during the year for standout defenseman Hy Buller. Bessette teamed with legendary netminder Johnny Bower to form the most formidable goaltending duo in professional hockey.

Pictured are 11 forwards from the 1941–1942 team that finished 33-19-4. From left to right are, (first row) Ed "Whitey" Prokop, Don Deacon, and Jake Milford; (second row) Joffre Desilets, Les Cunningham, and Norm Locking; (third row) Art Giroux, Earl Bartholomew, Alex "Bud" Cook, Walter Melnyk, and Herb Foster. After the season, the Barons received an invite to join the National Hockey League.

Terrance Caffery, a Cleveland center, fires the puck at Brian Cropper, goalie for the Tidewater Wings (Norfolk, Virginia) during this 1971–1972 regular season game. Caffery averaged over one point per game and would receive the Dudley "Red" Garrett outstanding rookie award in 1972.

A DYNASTY IS BORN

Posing comically are, from left to right, Fred Glover, Jack Gordon, and Eddie Olson, three of the Barons' most prolific scorers during the 1954–1955 season. Gordon took over as player/coach in 1956 and remained as head coach until 1968 when Glover was named player/coach. Olson left the Barons after the season after posting two straight 40-goal campaigns.

Barons center Ken Schultz gets checked hard into the boards by Pittsburgh Hornets defenseman Frank Mathers during a 4-0 Pittsburgh win in 1952. Mathers assumed the role of head coach of the Hershey Bears in 1956 and remained there until 1985, leading the Bears to three Calder Cup championships.

Barons defenseman Phil Samis unceremoniously removes Springfield center Kelly Burnett's skates from the ice during a 6-2 Cleveland win on November 14, 1950. After celebrating a Stanley Cup victory with the Toronto Maple Leafs in 1948, Samis played a significant role in helping the Barons capture the 1951 Calder Cup.

Center Jack Gordon (left) receives congratulations while holding the Calder Cup from head coach Frederick "Bun" Cook on April 16, 1953. One of the great head coaches in American Hockey League history, Cook guided Cleveland to five titles during his reign. Gordon later replaced Cook as the Barons' head man prior to the 1956–1957 season.

A DYNASTY IS BORN

Cleveland Browns Hall of Fame receiver Dante Lavelli eludes defenseman Ed Reigle of the Barons while scrimmaging in 1954. Lavelli, nicknamed "Glue Fingers," was a tremendous all-around athlete. In addition to a legendary football career and proficiency on the ice, he was offered a contract to play professional baseball as well.

Two of the greatest Barons of all time, a retired Fred Thurier (left) playfully reminds player/coach Jack Gordon which player compiled more career assists in February 1958. Gordon would eventually overtake Thurier, who ranks 23rd on the American Hockey League's all-time assist leaderboard and is now 20th on the list.

Head coach Jack Gordon gives a locker room pep talk to forward Bill Needham (No. 6), defensemen George Bouchard (No. 4), and Bob Robertson (No. 3) in 1959. Despite finishing with the league's second-best record, Gordon's Barons were upended by the lower-seeded Hershey Bears in a first-round playoff series.

A DYNASTY IS BORN

Barons coach Jack Gordon (back left) stands watch as goalie Johnny Albani dives for the puck in September 1958. Although he impressed a young Ken Dryden enough for the future hall-of-fame goalie to mention him in his book, Albani must not have performed well this day. He would only appear in three games for Cleveland.

A brawl during the February 19, 1958, game against the Hershey Bears leaves a post-apocalyptic scene at one end of the ice. The two most successful franchises in the history of the American Hockey League, the Barons and Bears, had a fierce rivalry. This night, Cleveland outslugged Hershey 2-0.

Cleveland's Bill Needham (No. 6) topples defenseman Bob Armstrong of the Springfield Indians during a 3-1 Barons loss on February 5, 1958. Armstrong played with Springfield briefly before playing in 542 games with the National Hockey League's Boston Bruins. He appeared in three Stanley Cup finals as well as the 1960 NHL All-Star Game.

Retired Baron Ed "Whitey" Prokop gives instruction to local amateur players in November 1959. Known for his quickness, Prokop played three years in Cleveland including the 1944–1945 championship season. Two years after leaving the Barons, Prokop scored 41 goals and dished out 39 assists in just 64 games for the Providence Reds.

A DYNASTY IS BORN

Cleveland's Ron Ingram delivers a hard check to center Willie Marshall of the Hershey Bears during a key playoff game in April 1957. Marshall retired in 1972 after 20 seasons in the American Hockey League and remains the all-time leader in every offensive category. He was inducted into the AHL Hall of Fame in 2006, and the league honors him each year by presenting the Willie Marshall Award to the season's top goal scorer. Ingram, a defenseman, only played 18 regular season games with the Barons but made a significant contribution during the 1957 title run. In 12 postseason contests, Ingram scored three goals and five assists as the Barons defeated Hershey and the Rochester Americans to win the city's eighth Calder Cup.

A scene difficult to fathom nowadays, fans are lined up before the box office even opens at 9:00 a.m. to purchase tickets for the 1948 American Hockey League playoffs. The Barons' 43-13-12 regular season record may have contributed to fan interest. Cleveland easily defeated the Providence Reds and Buffalo Bisons to win another Calder Cup.

Seen here is a rare look at empty seats inside the Cleveland Arena from 1950. The Barons routinely crammed larger-than-capacity crowds into the 10,000-seat building during the 1940s and 1950s. The arena was originally the brainchild of team owner Al Sutphin, who financed it during the Great Depression. The arena symbolized the glory years of hockey in Cleveland.

A DYNASTY IS BORN

A more common sight is a hockey game in the Cleveland Arena and not an empty seat to be seen. The arena also hosted basketball games, professional boxing and wrestling matches, six-day bicycle races, and Alan Freed's Moondog Coronation Ball. The arena became obsolete when the Coliseum in Richfield was built and was demolished 40 years after it opened.

Barons players must have felt they were in the Twilight Zone when they took the ice on November 29, 1950, to host the New Haven Eagles with only 1,640 people in the stands. The poor showing was due to problems with the city's public transportation, the primary method of attending games in those days.

Coach Jack Gordon addresses the troops prior to a game against the Springfield Indians on February 4, 1959. Barons players pictured at left from near to far are center Fred Glover, left wing Bob Barlow, right wing Bob Bailey, right wing Don Hogan, right wing Mike Ladadie, and right wing Cal Stearns. Seated at right is forward Bill Needham.

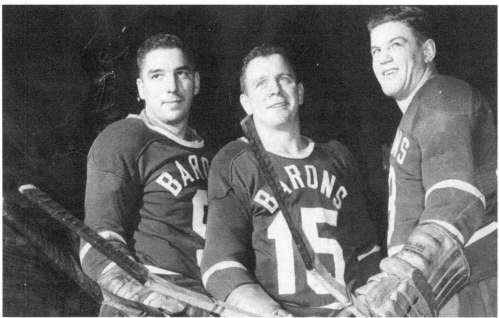

Cleveland's top three scorers in 1957—Fred Glover (left), Jimmy Moore (center), and Boris Elik—are pictured prior to a 3-2 loss to Springfield. Each player topped the 80-point mark during the regular season, leading the Barons to a championship. The dynamic line remained together for just one more season in Cleveland.

Pictured from left to right, Hershey Bears center Arnie Kullman, right wing Dunc Fisher, and goalies Gil Mayer and Bob Perreault take a casual stroll down Ontario Avenue in downtown Cleveland during a playoff series with the Barons in March 1959. Despite finishing with the fourth-best record in the American Hockey League and seven points behind the Barons, the Bears stunned Cleveland in seven games. The defeat was the second of five consecutive first-round playoff exits for the Barons. The Bears advanced to the finals where they defeated the Buffalo Bisons to win the Calder Cup. The championship was the second straight for Hershey and third overall for the franchise. Mayer, a five-time Harry Holmes Memorial Award winner for the goalie with lowest goals-against average, played for the Barons the following two seasons.

Cleveland star Fred Glover is dragged down by Providence Reds defenseman Bob Blackburn for a penalty as Providence netminder Ed Giacomin defends during a 5-0 Barons victory on March 25, 1964. The following month, the Barons won their ninth and final American Hockey League championship in spectacular fashion, sweeping the Rochester Americans, Hershey Bears, and Quebec Aces.

Cleveland players (from left to right) forward Bill Needham, defenseman Moe Mantha, coach Jack Gordon, and defenseman Aldo Guidolin talk strategy prior to a game with the Buffalo Bisons on November 11, 1960. The season ended in disappointment for the Barons in 1960 as they were swept in the first round of the playoffs by Springfield.

A DYNASTY IS BORN

New Barons (from left to right) defenseman Jacques Lemieux, goaltender Ernie Wakely, and center Gary Schall try to decipher a map of the city while resting in the terminal of Hopkins International Airport. The Barons spent most of the first month of the 1966 season on the road, not allowing the young players to familiarize themselves with their new hometown.

Right wing Cal Stearns and Barons general manager Jack Gordon give local celebrity Ron Penfound, host of the popular WEWS-TV television show "Captain Penny," some hockey tips on February 10, 1962. The 42-year-old Stearns played 70 games during the year and scored 42 points for the Barons.

New Barons (from left to right) goalie Gary Kurt, right wing Norm Beaudin, and defenseman Jim Watson discuss strategy with Cleveland head coach Jack Gordon in October 1969. The once dominant Barons slumped to 23-33-16 during the season and failed to make the playoffs. Kurt, Beaudin, and Watson would all spend significant time in the new World Hockey Association during the 1970s.

Cleveland's Bill Needham with his wife, Sue; daughter, Cheryl; and parents, Mr. and Mrs. George Needham, gather for a day in the Barons wing's honor in 1966. Needham played in Cleveland from 1956 to 1971 and was the Barons captain eight times. He played in 526 straight games and received the 1968 Eddie Shore Award as the American Hockey League's best defenseman.

A DYNASTY IS BORN

Barons player/coach Fred Glover (left) and defenseman Larry Zeidel go to great and hilarious lengths to prove that their reputations as the most notorious penalty offenders are undeserved in this 1966 photo opportunity. The statistics prove otherwise, however, as the duo is among the most penalized in American Hockey League history.

Goaltender Gerry Desjardins comes out of the crease to play the puck as Fred Glover assists during a 1967 game. Desjardins started 66 games for the Barons during the season and received the Dudley Garrett Memorial Award for the league's outstanding rookie. The netminder jumped to the National Hockey League, where he played 331 games for four different teams.

A scene right off the Donna Reed Show, Fred Glover and his wife celebrate as Glover is named player/coach of the Barons in June 1962 with team general manager Jack Gordon and his wife at the Gordons' house in Fairview Park. Looking through a scrapbook are children (from left to right) Jack Gordon Jr., Nancy Glover, and Janice Gordon.

Fred Glover is in action coaching a Barons practice. Glover left Cleveland after the 1967–1968 season to become a full-time head coach of the Oakland Seals of the National Hockey League. He did not enjoy as much success behind the bench as he did on the ice, posting a career NHL coaching record of 114-249-61.

There was nobody who displayed as much grit and determination on the ice as Fred Glover, the heart and soul of the Barons for most of two decades. He is shown here after a scuffle during a December 1967 game. Glover's younger brother Howie also played in Cleveland for six seasons.

Cleveland center Fred Glover and Springfield Kings defenseman Poul Popiel brawl during this December 1967 matchup. Players from near to far are Kings center Howie Menard, Barons defenseman Doug Piper, Kings left wing Doug Robinson, and Cleveland forward Jim Paterson. Official Tom Marer steps in to break it up.

From left to right, left wing Dick Van Impe, center Hank Ciesla, and defenseman Gary Bergman, all in their first season with Cleveland, pose together prior to the October 21, 1961, contest against the Buffalo Bisons. Cleveland would lose five of the next six meetings with Buffalo, who would go on to the Calder Cup finals.

Rochester defenseman Al Arbour and Cleveland forward Keith McCreary clash near the boards as the crowd looks on during game two of the AHL Championships. The Barons, down in the first period, would come back to win the May 5, 1966, contest 2-1 but not the series, sending the Calder Cup to the Americans.

The wild popularity of the Cleveland Barons ignited more interest in youth and recreational hockey leagues in northeast Ohio. Here, Clevelander Dick Hamevek (goalie) loses one into the net as Jack Matthews defends. Scoring the goal was Paul Brackenbush during a game in October 1960.

The Barons defensive line achieved the finest record in the AHL in the 1965–1966 season. Pictured from left to right are defensemen Larry Zeidel, Bill Speer, Ted Lanyon, goalie Les Binkley, defenseman Dick Mattinson, and center Bill Needham. In an odd coincidence, all five men lined up with Les Binkley shooting left-handed.

Barons center Garry Monahan (No. 10) is closed in on by Springfield's Jim Anderson (No. 10) and goalie Claude Hardy, but Monahan had already hit the cage for a second-period goal. The April 4, 1969, matchup would end in a 3-2 Barons victory. NHL veteran Monahan would return to the league permanently the next season.

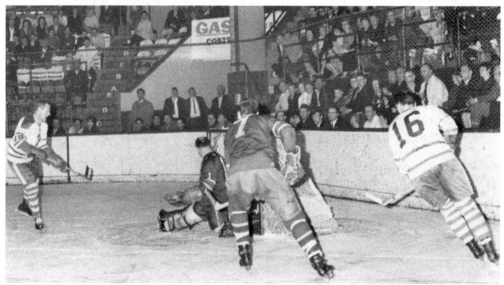

Barons forward Cecil Hoekstra (No. 19) scores the winning goal with a slapshot pass from Tom McCarthy (No. 16) with only 64 seconds left in the third period. Rochester Americans goalie Bob Perreault and Duane Rupp (No. 7) attempt the stop. The Barons won the May 5, 1966, game but lost the playoffs 4-2, giving Rochester the Calder Cup.

A DYNASTY IS BORN

Barons forward Norm Dennis (No. 10) and wing Bill Needham (No. 6) mix it up with Vancouver Canucks Tracy Pratt (No. 3). Goalie Gerry Desjardin looks on as Needham and Pratt drew penalties in the November 3, 1967, game. In the 1965 through 1967 seasons, the Western Hockey League and the AHL played an interlocking schedule.

During the first game of the playoffs, Howie Glover intercepted the puck at center ice, then skated above Pittsburgh goalie George Gardener to draw him out. This goal in the third period would make the score 5-1. The Barons would win the April 13, 1966, matchup 5-2 and take the series 3-0.

Barons goalie Gary Kurt knocks the puck away and makes a save on the shot by Bears center Michel Harvey. The Barons would allow four goals on the night causing them to fall 4-2 to Hershey in the March 24, 1971, matchup. The Bears would later fall to Cleveland in the playoffs.

Proving that hockey players can also have an artistic side, Fred Glover, Gus Karrys, and Ray Ross are seen painting in this January 19, 1954, photograph. Despite two five-plus-game losing streaks in the season, the Barons would go on to a 38-32-0 season and win the Calder Cup.

A DYNASTY IS BORN

Barons center Gord Labossiere (No. 22) mixes it up with Cincinnati defenseman Chris Evans (No. 7) as Swords goalie Norm "Rocky" Farr falls on a loose puck during this October 13, 1971, contest. The Swords won the game 3-2. When the teams met again two days later, the Barons would again be cut down by the Swords in a 4-3 battle. This was the inaugural season for the short-lived Cincinnati Swords, who played only two more seasons before folding. It would be more than 20 years before the city would have another AHL team, the Cincinnati Mighty Ducks. The Swords made playoff appearances in two of three seasons, winning the Calder cup in their second season. Despite a winning season and another playoff appearance, the team folded after its third season, unable to compete with the newly formed WHA team, the Cincinnati Stingers.

Barons Barrie Meissner whoops it up as the winning goal is scored by fellow forward Mike Chernoff (not pictured). Looking on in shock are Quebec Aces defensemen Ralph MacSweyn (No. 4) and goalie Mike Belhumeur. The Barons took the December 2, 1970, game 4-2. Both teams were ousted from the playoffs by the Springfield Kings.

Pictured from left to right, president John Karr, general manager Harry Howell, and trainer Gerry Dean are at a reception held on May 11, 1978, to welcome Howell and Dean back from Team Canada play. Howell coached the Canadian national team, and Dean was a trainer. The team took bronze at the World Championships in Prague, Czechoslovakia.

A DYNASTY IS BORN

Darryl Sly (No. 9) of Rochester sprawls on top of Barons forward Bill Orban as both watch the puck bounce free. It would be a Barons win as they sent the Americans home 2-1 on the evening of February 21, 1971. This was Bill Orban's first and only season with the Barons.

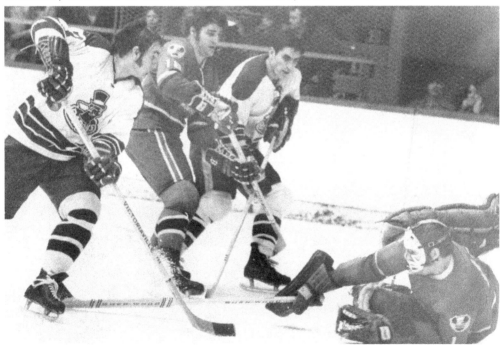

Goalie Ken Dryden of the Montreal Voyageurs dives on the ice, putting an end to a drive by Barons Mike Chernoff and Norm Beaudin. The teams skated to a 2-2 tie. One of the all-time greats, Dryden is also known for providing color commentary during the 1980 "Miracle on Ice" Olympic game, with the United States victors over the Soviet Union.

Seen at left, empty seats were typical during the 1972–1973 season for the Barons as the new WHL Crusaders took the choice game dates and the fans jumped on the "major league" bandwagon. The last home game before the team's mid-season move to Jacksonville was this 5-1 loss to Richmond on February 4, 1973. It drew an abysmal 435 fans. Below, in the arena's south lobby, a closeout sale offered Barons souvenir items marked down. Attendance that season was the lowest in Barons history, with games drawing as few as 240 fans, leaving the once beloved franchise no choice but to say goodbye.

A DYNASTY IS BORN

2

MAJOR LEAGUE HOCKEY
ARRIVES IN CLEVELAND

Nick Mileti was never a minor-league kind of guy. Having brought big-league basketball to Cleveland with his Cavaliers in 1970, Mileti had similar intentions with hockey. Always a staunch supporter of Cleveland, Mileti saw no reason the city could not support four major-league sports franchises.

Unfortunately, the National Hockey League was an exclusive club and did not appear interested in affording Mileti membership. Undaunted, he then set his sights on the upstart World Hockey Association.

In Cleveland, Nick Mileti was approved a franchise by the WHA and was awarded the defunct Calgary Broncos, who were forced to fold before ever taking the ice. After the name "Crusaders" was picked by readers of a local newspaper, Cleveland officially had its first major league hockey team.

While WHA teams began luring big-name NHL stars with salary increases and greater contractual freedom, Mileti recognized the need for the Crusaders to have their own star centerpiece. He eventually got it by inking Boston Bruins goaltender Gerry Cheevers to a contract with the Crusaders. Widely considered one of the best netminders in the game, Cheevers had just led Boston to Stanley Cup championships in two of the previous three seasons and was a legitimate superstar.

The "Purple Gang," as they would come to be called, officially opened on October 11, 1972, at the Cleveland Arena. A lively crowd of 9,681 showed up to see the hometown boys host the Quebec Nordiques, coached by Montreal Canadien legend Maurice "Rocket" Richard. The Cleveland bench was led by former Cleveland Baron Bill Needham. Gerry Cheevers immediately proved his worth, shutting out the Nordiques and securing the first victory in Crusaders history, 2-0.

By the end of the first month of the season, it was clear the Crusaders were among the elite in the WHA, at 7-2-1. The Crusaders finished the season just like they started, with a five-game win streak. Their final record of 43-32-3 and 89 points was good enough for third best in the 12-team league.

Unfortunately, the Crusaders would never again enjoy a season quite like the first. The team dipped to third in the Eastern Division in the 1973–1974 season and was ousted by the Toronto Toros in the first round of the playoffs.

The 1974–1975 campaign, the Crusaders' third in Cleveland, was seemingly doomed from the start. Scheduled to move home games from the Cleveland Arena to the new Coliseum in Richfield, the Crusaders had trouble actually playing opening night. Due to a problem with the ice surface, the game actually had to be rescheduled twice, sending thousands of fans home disgusted.

Midway through the season, the organization decided to fire coach John Hanna and replace him on the bench with general manager Jack Vivian. To make matters worse, in what would become a recurring theme for Cleveland hockey fans during the 1970s, the Crusaders' financial difficulties began to manifest.

With the organization on the verge of financial collapse, Nick Mileti announced the sale of controlling interest of the team to local businessman Jay P. Moore in early March. The Crusaders limped to the finish line with their worst record in three seasons. While they again qualified for the WHA playoffs, the Purple Gang was easily bounced by the superior Houston Aeros.

The 1975–1976 season would be the final one for the Crusaders in Cleveland, and it resembled more of a soap opera than a professional hockey campaign. With the team playing at a mediocre level under new coach Johnny Wilson, management attempted to light a spark with several personnel moves. The most notable was the demotion to the minor leagues and subsequent trade of the very popular and original Crusader Wayne Muloin.

The team suffered a dismal 3-11 December as fan interest waned. As the organization's financial crisis peaked, player paychecks began to arrive late and the ones that did arrive were not clearing. Desperate to keep the ship afloat, the Crusaders worked out a deal with goalie Gerry Cheevers to release him from his contract. The deal would save the franchise money, but the blow to team morale was undeniable.

As if the chasm between players and management was not great enough, word spread in early March of a trip team owner Jay Moore and general manager Jack Vivian took to Kansas City. Crusaders brass met with ownership of the NHL's Kansas City Scouts, struggling just as bad as the Crusaders, to negotiate a deal to merge the franchises as an NHL team in Cleveland.

Not aware of the depth of the team's fiscal troubles, players and fans revolted against the front office. Players decided to wear black arm bands for their March 10 contest with the Cincinnati Stingers at the Coliseum. Fans showed up and offered full support to the players. A contentious meeting with management and players led to the resignation of Jack Vivian. With all the drama in Cleveland, the deal with the Kansas City Scouts, which was tentatively approved by the NHL, fell through. The Scouts instead moved to Denver and became the Colorado Rockies

Once the Kansas City deal collapsed and a separate group began working to bring the California Golden Seals to Cleveland, the fate of the Crusaders was set. The team finished the season, and although they still managed to qualify for the playoffs, they were easily swept by the New England Whalers. The final Crusaders game in Cleveland was played on April 11, 1976.

After the season, the Crusaders struck a deal with ownership of the defunct Minnesota Fighting Saints to merge the franchises and compete again in Minnesota. Not long after, the WHA began to take on water and the league started talks with the NHL. The WHA finished the 1978–1979 season with just six teams. After extensive negotiations with the NHL, four of the WHA's teams—the Edmonton Oilers, Quebec Nordiques, Winnipeg Jets, and New England (renamed Hartford) Whalers—were absorbed into the NHL.

Pictured is a model of the Cleveland Cavaliers and Barons owner Nick Mileti's proposed new arena in rural Richfield, Ohio, from 1971. With the Cleveland Arena aging, too small, and lacking adequate parking, Mileti sought to put his facility far away from downtown Cleveland where parking and city congestion would not be such a hindrance. Also, with the arena positioned between Cleveland and Akron, events would draw fans from both metropolitan areas.

Above, foundation is laid for the new Coliseum in Richfield, Ohio, a scant 45-minute drive from downtown Cleveland. The Coliseum was the brainchild of Nick Mileti, who needed a new home for his basketball Cavaliers and hockey Crusaders. At left, there was embarrassment all around on October 30, 1974, as the brand-new arena betrayed Mileti (center) and Crusaders general manager Jack Vivian (right)—a problem with a pipe under the ice surface forced the Crusaders' much-anticipated opener to be postponed not once, but twice.

Cleveland became a major league hockey town during this June 1972 press conference. Gary Davidson, founder and president of the World Hockey Association, makes it official with the new team's owner, Nick Mileti. Davidson also helped create the American Basketball Association. Cleveland would assume the spot vacated by the Calgary Broncos, who never got off the ground in the WHA.

Crusaders and Cleveland Cavaliers owner Nick Mileti holds a press conference to announce the signing of goalie Gerry Cheevers. The superstar Cheevers led the Boston Bruins to a Stanley Cup title the previous season in the National Hockey League and immediately gave Cleveland an identity.

Nick Mileti (center) stands with new head coach Bill Needham (left) and prize signing Gerry Cheevers. The beloved Needham played nearly 1,000 games in a Barons uniform, and along with Cheevers, was expected to be the cornerstone on which Mileti could build his franchise.

Cleveland goaltender Gerry Cheevers plays the puck as defenseman Ray Clearwater supports from the back side. Cheevers was the face of the franchise during his time in Cleveland. He played 191 games for the Crusaders over four years, posting a win-loss record of 99-78-9. He was a three-time World Hockey Association All-Star and led the league with a 2.84 goals against average for the 1972–1973 season. Cheevers recorded 14 shutouts for Cleveland, leading the WHA three of his four seasons. The goalie returned to the Boston Bruins of the National Hockey League after the Crusaders folded, playing four more seasons. He retired from the NHL with a 230-102-74 record and was subsequently inducted into the Hockey Hall of Fame in 1985.

Head coach Bill Needham observes the action during a 1972 Crusaders game at the Cleveland Arena. Needham guided the club to playoff appearances in the first two seasons and compiled an 80-64-12 record. Nonetheless, he was fired after two seasons as the Crusaders' top man. Seated in front of Needham are left wing Gary Jarrett (left) and center Ron Buchanan.

Star defenseman Paul Shmyr celebrates Gary Jarrett's goal on Quebec Nordiques goalie Michel Deguise during a 1973 game. Shmyr was a stalwart for the Crusaders, who acquired him after he spent time with the Chicago Blackhawks and California Golden Seals. Shmyr was recognized with the Dennis A. Murphy Trophy as top World Hockey Association defenseman in 1976.

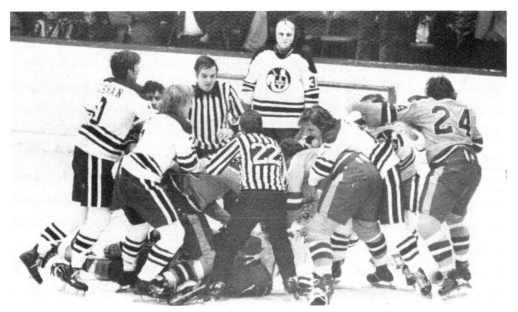

Gerry Cheevers watches casually as Cleveland Crusaders and New York Raiders skaters brawl in front of him. Ironically, Cheevers started the fracas by poking Raiders left wing Craig Reichmuth with his stick. Cleveland won the game 4-3 in overtime on October 17, 1972. The Crusaders beat New York again two days later for a perfect 5-0 start to their inaugural season.

Crusaders players get into the Christmas spirit by mixing it up with the Houston Aeros during a 3-0 loss on December 22, 1974. The dominant Aeros finished 53-25 during the regular season and cruised to an AVCO Cup title. The Crusaders were the only opponent to even win a playoff game against Houston.

Brothers Wayne (left) and Larry Hillman from Kirkland Lake, Ontario, defend together during a 3-2 Crusaders victory over the Winnipeg Jets in 1975. The Hillman brothers played two seasons together in Cleveland after long NHL careers. Though both were in their mid-30s, the Hillmans were acquired because of their experience as Cleveland tried to build up the blue line and better support goalie Gerry Cheevers. Both brothers left the Crusaders just prior to the team's final season in 1975. Larry Hillman played on six Stanley Cup–winning teams with three different franchises. He is the youngest player ever to have his name engraved on the trophy when he won it with the Detroit Red Wings in 1955. Sadly, Wayne Hillman died of cancer in 1990 at just 52 years old.

The great Bobby Hull of the Winnipeg Jets skates around Cleveland's Grant Erickson during a 4-2 Crusader triumph on March 30, 1973. Hull stunned the hockey world when he jumped from the National Hockey League to Winnipeg, giving the World Hockey Association instant credibility. He topped the 50-goal mark in each of his first four seasons, scoring an amazing 77 goals in 1974–1975.

A Cleveland fan tries to taunt hockey legend Gordie Howe with a rubber chicken before the Crusaders take on the Houston Aeros on March 20, 1974. After playing with the Detroit Red Wings from 1946 to 1971, Howe joined the Aeros at age 45 and produced 301 points in his first three seasons, leading Houston to two AVCO Cup championships.

Cleveland left wing Grant Erickson and Alberta Oiler Bob Wall battle each other on the ice during a 5-4 Crusaders win on February 20, 1973. Erickson was a familiar face for local hockey fans as he skated for the American Hockey League's Barons from 1970 to 1972. He played three seasons for the Crusaders, enjoying his best in 1973–1974, scoring 23 goals and dishing out 27 assists.

Michigan Stags Randy Legge hurdles Cleveland left wing Gary Jarrett during a 1974 game. Jarrett had a tremendous first season with the Crusaders, leading the 1972–1973 team with 40 goals. He also scored eight goals in nine games in the playoffs. Defenseman Legge became a Crusader the following season.

Defenseman Blake Ball (No. 8) and center Ron Buchanan assist goaltender Gerry Cheevers during a playoff game in 1973. Cheevers's famous mask included a stitch painted on every time the netminder took a puck to the face. While Cheevers signing in 1972 was a great moment for the local hockey community, his departure was bitter and sad. With the franchise going broke and desperate to get out from his large contract, the organization began a smear campaign against the goalie. At the same time, Cheevers gave some of his own money to help cover player paychecks, which were routinely late and would sometimes bounce. Eventually, the two sides agreed on a buyout deal and Cheevers was released from his contract before the 1975–1976 season ended. He was sorely missed. It was the beginning of the end of Crusaders hockey in northeast Ohio.

With goalie Gerry Cheevers out of position, Cleveland defenseman Ray Clearwater robs Philadelphia left wing Don Herriman of a goal to help preserve a 5-3 Crusader win on February 2, 1973. Two months later, the Crusaders swept the Blazers in four games to earn the only playoff series win of their existence.

Crusaders center Ron Buchanan battles Philadelphia Blazers right wing John McKenzie during the first game of a playoff series in 1973. Buchanan would score the winning goal in overtime, giving Cleveland a 3-2 victory. McKenzie, who played 1,168 career big-league games between the National Hockey League and World Hockey Association, scored both goals for the Blazers.

Baltimore Blades center J.P. LeBlanc loses a glove during a scuffle with Cleveland defenseman Larry Hillman during a March 1975 game. The Blades began the season as the Michigan Stags playing in Detroit. When the Stags folded in January, the league took control of the franchise and moved it to Baltimore to become the Blades. The Blades also folded after the season.

Right wing Terry Holbrook signs with general manager Jack Vivian and the Crusaders in May 1974 after playing the previous two seasons with the Minnesota North Stars. Ironically, Holbrook played for the Barons of the American Hockey League for three seasons and was on the 1972–1973 team that was driven out of Cleveland by the arrival of the Crusaders.

Crusader Ron Buchanan scores the third of a four-goal night on November 16, 1972, embarrassing Ottawa Nationals and former Cleveland Baron netminder Les Binkley. Cleveland won the game 6-3. The Nationals lasted only one season in the World Hockey Association and became the Toronto Toros. Three years later, the Toros became the Birmingham Bulls.

Cleveland goalie Gerry Cheevers lays out in an attempt to make a stop on Winnipeg Jets defenseman Larry Hornung's shot as Jets right wing Howie Young goes airborne. The Crusaders won the game 3-2 on February 5, 1975. Winnipeg was the most successful World Hockey Association team, winning three of the seven league championships.

Skip Krake flips a shot at Alberta Oilers goalie Ken Brown as leading goal-scorer Gary Jarrett positions for a rebound during a 6-0 Cleveland win on October 27, 1972. The Oilers, later called "Edmonton," are the last original WHA team still in existence.

A common occurrence, Gerry Cheevers comes out of the net to make a play on New England Whaler Tom Webster as Crusader Bill Horton defends during a playoff series in 1973 that was won by New England. Webster posted a 103-point season in 1972–1973 as the Whalers won the first AVCO Cup championship.

Chicago Cougars goaltender Dave Dryden, brother of legend Ken Dryden, pokes the stick at Crusader Grant Erickson's skates during a 5-3 Cleveland win on February 12, 1975. An arguably cursed World Hockey Association franchise, the Cougars squeaked into the playoffs in 1974. Unfortunately, a touring production of Peter Pan apparently did not expect the Cougars to get past the New England Whalers in their first-round playoff series and booked the Cougars' ancient home arena, the International Amphitheatre. Desperate for somewhere to play their semifinal

MAJOR LEAGUE HOCKEY ARRIVES IN CLEVELAND

series, the Cougars considered playing in the Cleveland Arena before turning to a public skating rink in Mount Pleasant, Illinois. Embarrassingly, only 2,000 fans could fit into the Randhurst Ice Arena (now a Home Depot) to watch the Cougars beat Toronto. With the Cougars playing in the finals and Peter Pan flying away to another city, all appeared well until it was revealed that amphitheatre staff had inexplicably melted the ice and dismantled cooling pipes, sending the Cougars back to the mall skating rink.

A chalkboard shows the starting lineups for a Crusaders game seemingly frozen in time as items are auctioned off from the Cleveland Arena floor in April 1976. The facility was once an American hockey palace, featuring one of the largest seating capacities at the time it opened in 1937. It was as much responsible for the glory days of Cleveland hockey as the teams that played in it. Unlike in the 1940s and 1950s, however, fans no longer relied solely on public transportation to get to and from sporting events. Along with a suddenly small seating capacity, the parking availability at the arena was atrocious. The building of the Coliseum in Richfield, Ohio, in 1974 remedied all of these ills and quickly made the old arena obsolete. The arena quickly deteriorated and was demolished in 1977. Today, the site is occupied by a Red Cross building.

Local businessman Jay P. Moore (middle) is all smiles after purchasing the Crusaders from Nick Mileti (right) on March 3, 1975. Moore's elation would be short-lived upon the realization of the debt the franchise was buried under. After an attempt to merge with a National Hockey League team failed a year later, the Crusaders eventually merged with the defunct Minnesota Fighting Saints and folded in January 1977.

The Cleveland Arena is turned into rubble in April 1977. A place where hockey once thrived and the first home of the Crusaders, the arena was left without a purpose after the Richfield Coliseum became operational. Hockey was never the same at the Coliseum, as two major league teams were dissolved in a three-year span at the building.

Fans and players both turned on team management when news broke of a deal to merge the Crusaders with the National Hockey League's Kansas City Scouts. The deal would result in an NHL team in Cleveland to replace the Crusaders. One of the largest and most passionate crowds turned out for a protest game with the Cincinnati Stingers. The Cleveland players wore black arm bands and fans dressed in all black as a show of support. What fans did not know was that the Crusaders, like the NHL's Scouts, were on the brink of financial collapse. With all the controversy the story stirred up, the Kansas City deal fell through and the Scouts went to Denver to become the Colorado Rockies. Eventually, the Rockies became the New Jersey Devils. The collapse of the proposed merger also spelled doom for the Crusaders, who already existed on borrowed time.

MAJOR LEAGUE HOCKEY ARRIVES IN CLEVELAND

3

THE NHL BARONS

It has often been said that timing is everything. For the city of Cleveland, the timing could not have been worse to get its first crack at the National Hockey League. After decades of trying to join professional hockey's big boy club, the dream appeared to become reality just prior to the 1976–1977 season.

While the Crusaders were going down in flames, the NHL's California Golden Seals were suffering the same fate in the Bay Area. Brothers and Cleveland natives George and Gordon Gund were minority owners of the Seals. George Gund convinced primary owner Melvin Swig to move the franchise to their hometown to play in the Richfield Coliseum. The Coliseum, with its large seating capacity, was a major factor in the NHL approving the move in July 1976. Ironically, it would be the Coliseum's location that played a role in the franchise's ultimate demise.

Just like that, Cleveland had an NHL hockey team, which was named the "Barons" in a nod to the legendary AHL team. Unfortunately, the move from California was hurried and made out of financial necessity rather than sound logic. The Barons were going to share the Coliseum with a basketball team that had captured the city's heart mere months prior.

In just their sixth season in the National Basketball Association, the Cavaliers won the Eastern Conference's Central Division with a 49-33 record. In what would come to be known as the "Miracle of Richfield," the Cavs defeated the Washington Bullets four games to three in the conference semifinals. The 87-85 win in game seven of the series was so thrilling that fans at the Coliseum stormed the court after the final buzzer and actually pulled down one of the basket supports.

A basketball-crazed town was not exactly the ideal climate to introduce a floundering, no-name hockey team into. To make matters worse, the cash-strapped Barons lacked the resources to adequately promote the team leading up to the season. It was little surprise that only 8,899 fans turned out for the team's opener on October 6, 1976, versus the Los Angeles Kings.

The Barons were a team that needed to win early and often to establish themselves with the northeast Ohio sports fan. Unfortunately, the roster did not contain enough talent to do so. After a loss to the Buffalo Sabres on December 8, the Barons fell to a dismal 6-15-7. With a brutal winter pummeling the region with snow and the team buried in last place, most fans saw little reason to trek to rural Richfield for a hockey game. Meanwhile, the Cavs were on their way to another playoff appearance and would finish fourth in the NBA in attendance.

If the Barons' performance on the ice was bad, the performance of ownership was worse. In a cruel dose of déjà vu, word broke that another Cleveland hockey team would fail to make payroll. With Cleveland players once again having to worry about so much more than just winning hockey games, Mel Swig appealed to the NHL for a loan to help the franchise finish the season. Eventually, the NHL Players' Association stepped in with a loan to ensure the Barons would stay afloat the rest of the season.

As for what happened on the ice, the Barons limped to the finish line with a 25-42-13 record, good for last in the Adams Division and 18 points behind third-place Toronto. After the season, Mel Swig finally had enough and sold the controlling interest of the club to the Gunds.

With the staggering amounts of money the franchise was losing, the Barons needed to capture the community's attention during the 1977–1978 season. The problem was the roster had not changed much from the previous year and to expect drastically different results was foolish. The Cavaliers continued to play winning basketball, the Cleveland winter continued to pound the region with snow, and the Barons remained an afterthought.

Nonetheless, the Barons came upon a couple of opportunities to turn things around during that second season in Cleveland. The first came the night of November 23, 1977, when the mighty Montreal Canadiens came to town. Most likely, the majority of the 12,859 fans who attended the game did so to see Montreal, rather than the 5-10-2 Barons. In the third year of a four-year run of Stanley Cups, these Canadiens were the finest team the NHL had ever seen. They had only lost eight games in regulation the previous season. Montreal's roster included a mind-boggling nine future hall-of-famers!

The previous season, Montreal soundly defeated the Barons during all five meetings. There was no reason to expect anything different this night. Shockingly, the Barons stunned the visitors 2-1 in front of a raucous crowd. It was a rare, big night for the Barons. However, when the team dropped their next three games, the Montreal win appeared to be nothing more than a fluke.

The Barons had one final chance to earn a permanent place in Cleveland. With the team sputtering and leaking oil in early January, general manager Harry Howell determined it was time to act. With a pair of four-player trades, Howell acquired veterans J.P. Parise, Jean Potvin, and Chuck Arnason, as well as tough-guy Rick Jodzio.

The moves appeared to have an immediate impact as the Barons posted wins in the next three games. The revamped roster held steady through the rest of January. Following a 2-0 victory over Detroit on February 1, the Barons were a respectable 18-30-4 and within striking distance of a playoff run. The community took notice. A franchise-high 13,110 people filled the Coliseum on February 4 to see the team skate to a 2-2 tie with the Philadelphia Flyers. The team faced a genuine opportunity to build some momentum.

Then the unthinkable happened.

Between February 5 and March 25, the Barons hit an abysmal stretch of hockey that reached epic proportions. Going just 1-13-7, any hopes of competing for the playoffs or building a semblance of fan support went out the window. It was a devastating stretch that sealed the fate of NHL hockey in Cleveland forever.

The team played out the season and finished 22-45-13, worse than the previous season. Also worse was attendance, which dipped to 5,676 a game from 6,194 the year before. Suffering steep financial losses, the Gunds abandoned the dream of a thriving NHL team in Cleveland and arranged a deal to merge the Barons with the Minnesota North Stars. The two teams merged in Minnesota and remained the North Stars. Not since the Barons has an American professional sports franchise in one of the big four sports leagues ceased operations.

It was a sad and bitter ending to a team that never really had a chance. Worse, for the first time since the late 1920s, there was no professional hockey team representing Cleveland. It would be nearly two decades before the city would enjoy another one.

Seen above is a perfect juxtaposition of rural and urban as cattle casually graze just outside where tens of thousands of people convene for sporting events and concerts. Below, the Coliseum was a spectacular sight to see sitting amongst the backdrop of nature and wildlife. The building at 2923 Streetsboro Road in Richfield opened in 1974 with a Frank Sinatra concert. While parking was plentiful outside the Coliseum, getting there was not so easy with only one highway leading Clevelanders to Richfield. Traffic jams often caused fans to arrive late to events.

Above, the signature mustard-colored seats are pictured inside the Richfield Coliseum. Fans sat here to witness the March 24, 1975, boxing match between Muhammed Ali and Chuck Wepner. Wepner's performance that night inspired actor Sylvester Stallone to write the script for the movie *Rocky*. Below, the goal horn is disassembled after a Cleveland Barons game with the fearsome Montreal Canadiens. Although three different hockey teams played in the Coliseum, basketball was far and away the more popular draw. Many still speculate what the fate of the Barons might have been had they played downtown. The Coliseum was demolished in 1999, just 25 years after the doors opened.

THE NHL BARONS

Cleveland Baron Dennis Maruk leaps over the stick of St. Louis Blues center Gordon "Red" Berenson. Nobody provided more thrills for fans during the Barons' short NHL stint in Cleveland than Maruk. The diminutive player scored 64 goals and 149 points during his two seasons in Cleveland. He was the last Cleveland Baron to play in the NHL when he retired from the Minnesota North Stars in 1989 with 356 career goals. Maruk also netted a 60-goal campaign in 1981–1982 while playing with the Washington Capitals.

Barons defensemen Len Frig and Greg Smith battle for the puck with Canadiens forward Guy Lafleur in this February 1, 1977, contest. Montreal won every matchup with Cleveland during the 1977–1978 season. Led by famed coach William "Scotty" Bowman, the Canadiens would go on to win the Stanley Cup.

Kings defenseman Larry Brown checks Barons forward Dennis Maruk with his stick, sending him crashing onto the ice and drawing a penalty for cross-checking in the first period of this February 9, 1977, matchup. Cleveland would skate to its first victory over Los Angeles all season, doubling up the Kings 6-3.

St. Louis Blues center Larry Patey gets the puck past Barons goalie Gary Simmons but misses the cage. The October 21, 1976, contest ended with a 6-2 Cleveland victory. Simmons, new to Cleveland, would remain with the Barons only part of the season before being traded to the Los Angeles Kings.

The matchup on February 9, 1977, between the Cleveland Barons and Los Angeles Kings continues to get chippy in the first period. Barons defenseman and NHL rookie Greg Smith lands a left hook to the chin of helmetless Kings forward Dave "The Hammer" Schultz and looks to land a right as well.

Barons defenseman Greg Smith (No. 5), goalie Gilles Meloche, and North Stars forward Tim Young watch as the puck bounces away during this March 17, 1978, matchup. Occurring in the days before shootouts, the teams came away with a 4-4 tie.

Ice sprays as Sabres center Gilbert Perreault and goalie Gilles Meloche end up in a tangle on the ice. In the background, Barons defenseman Mike Christie skates in. Cleveland would lose the sparsely attended December 8, 1976, meeting to Buffalo, 5-1, capping a three-game losing streak for the Barons.

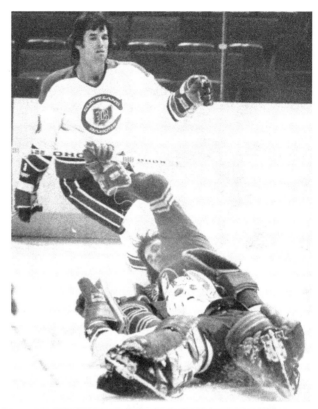

Cleveland Barons (from left to right) defenseman Mike Christie, center Dave Gardner, and defenseman Rick Hampton chase down Red Wing Dennis Hextall for control of the puck while Detroit forward Bill Lochead tumbles to the ice. Both teams struggled through the 1976–1977 season with low win totals and attendance.

Barons goalie Gary Edwards gets an encouraging pat on the head from forward Brent Meeke after shutting out the Pittsburgh Penguins in a scoreless tie. Edwards was acquired midseason from the Los Angeles Kings. Cleveland would not defeat the Penguins in any of the five regular season matchups.

Referees attempt to slow the melee as more than a half-dozen players from the Montreal Canadiens and the Cleveland Barons lock up in a brawl at the Barons net. The 8-1 loss during the November 24, 1976, game would leave Cleveland demoralized; it would be weeks before the Barons won again.

THE NHL BARONS

Cleveland defenseman James "Jim" Neilson, seen playing in his 1,000th NHL game, helps out goalie Gilles Meloche as the Islanders close in. Cleveland fell to New York 5-3 in the January 7, 1978, game. The Islanders were a formidable opponent even for a defenseman, boasting league leaders in goals, assists, and points that season. Neilson, known as "Chief," learned to play hockey while growing up in an orphanage in Saskatchewan. He spent most of his career with the New York Rangers.

Barons defenseman Len Frig gets his stick across the ankles of Pittsburgh Penguins left wing Mike Corrigan, who swiftly passes off the puck. Both Frig and Corrigan would spend only the 1976–1977 season with their respective teams. Despite intense play, the February 3, 1977, battle would end with a 0-0 tie.

Cleveland forward Al MacAdam eyes the flying puck as Kings defenseman Dave Hutchinson follows in close pursuit. In the background, Dennis Maruk (No. 21) skates toward the pair. MacAdam and Maruk were well traveled as members of the former California Seals and would be moved again in two seasons to the Minnesota North Stars.

Friends and teammates Cleveland defenseman Jim Neilson and goalie Gilles Meloche skate off the ice together. Meloche helped lead the team to victory by shutting out the Chicago Black Hawks 3-0 in the October 19, 1976, matchup. Neilson and Meloche had also made the move together from California to Cleveland.

The first Barons goal is scored by forward Al MacAdam as he fires the puck through the legs of Detroit Red Wings goalie Ed Giacomin in the second period of play. This preseason game offered a brief period of hope for two of the league's worst teams during the 1976–1977 season.

Surrounded by teammates, Rick Hampton (above) rises to acknowledge his introduction at the October 11, 1977, Barons team luncheon. The next night, the team would kick off the season with a 2-0 loss to the Los Angeles Kings. The first home game, however, would give the fans a moment of hope as it kicked off a four-game win streak that would, unfortunately, be the longest of the season. At left, defenseman Mike Christie and forward Al MacAdam look weary and unenthused as they disembark from the wayward bus that caused them to be late for the Barons' luncheon.

The stern look on this mannequin's face could possibly be an attempt to conceal tears. With the completion of the Barons' second NHL season came the announcement that the team would dissolve into the Minnesota North Stars for the 1978–1979 season. The Barons remain the last American major-league sports team to cease operations.

Defenseman Jim Neilson and goalie Gary Simmons talk to the press after returning from a 4-3 loss to the Bruins in Boston on October 10, 1976. Simmons would spend only a half dozen games with the Barons before being traded to the Los Angeles Kings for fellow goalie Gary Edwards.

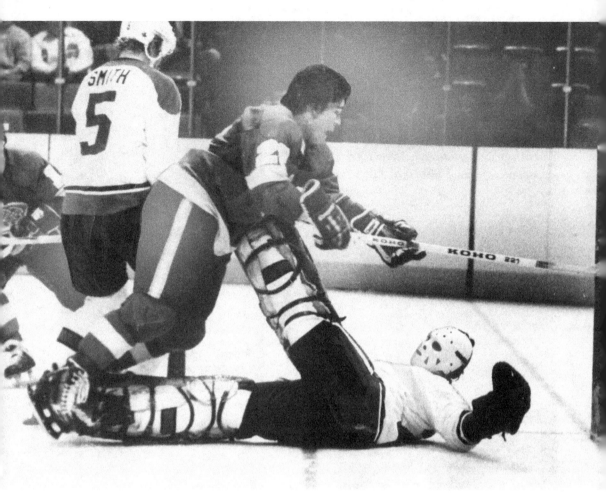

There would be no winners or losers for the franchise opener on October 6, 1976. In the final moments of the Barons' first NHL game, Los Angeles Kings defenseman Gary Sargent drives in on Cleveland goalie Gilles Meloche, who turned away the shot to preserve the 2-2 score. Sargent, a full-blooded Native American Chippewa, was a well-rounded athlete who turned down a major league baseball contract and two football scholarships to become a hockey player.

THE NHL BARONS

New York Rangers defenseman Carol Vadnais shoves Barons forward Dennis Maruk out of the way as he assists Rangers goalie Wayne Thomas. New York's defense would remain dominant throughout the night, and the October 25, 1977, contest would end in a one-sided 5-0 shutout for the Rangers.

Barons left wing Mike Fidler blasts a puck point blank, but Bruins goalie and former Crusaders legend Gerry Cheevers makes the save. The December 28, 1977, matchup would end in a 5-5 tie. After leaving Cleveland, Cheevers returned to the NHL and Boston for five seasons before retiring.

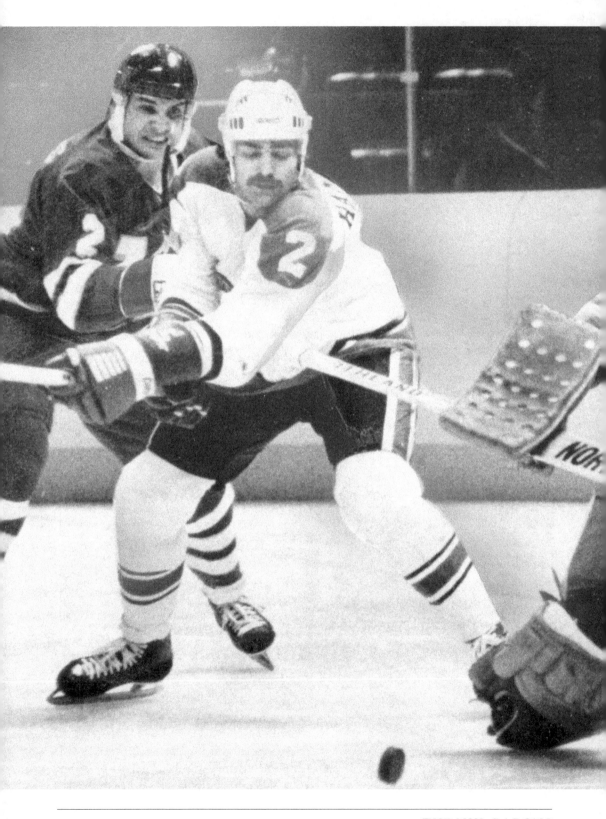

THE NHL BARONS

Barons defenseman Rick
Hampton tries to beat
North Stars goalie Pete
LoPresti to the puck
while avoiding a check by
Minnesota defenseman
Bill Butters. Cleveland
would take the game 7-3.
The following season, the
two struggling teams would
merge in Minnesota under
the North Stars name.

With members of the Barons looking on, NHL player's attorney Alan Eagleson tells newsmen that the Barons players would do a mass "retirement" before the night's game against Buffalo, unless the players' salaries were guaranteed for the rest of the season. Cleveland would play and lose the February 23, 1977, match 5-3. Financial difficulties plagued the franchise from its days in Oakland as the Golden Seals, and there were serious questions whether the Barons would actually finish the year. After the season, owner Mel Swig sold the team to George and Gordon Gund.

The view from the loge level of the January 12, 1978, Barons game against Buffalo was sweetened by the Cleveland offense during a 6-3 victory. Unfortunately, just 2,110 fans got to witness the victory, a rarity during the 1977–1978 season when the team won just 22 games.

As his teammates look on, Cleveland forward Jim Pappin fires at the net but Chicago goalie Tony Esposito manages to make the save. This stop came in the second period of the October 19, 1977, contest against the Black Hawks. The Barons won the game 3-0.

Cleveland defenseman Rick Hampton fires a puck as Kings goalie Rogatien Vachon defends on the play. The shot narrowly missed the cage. Los Angeles would give up two goals before the night was over, but with the Barons defense allowing four, Cleveland fell to the Kings again.

Barons goalie Gilles Meloche skillfully deflects a shot by Philadelphia Flyers left wing Bob Kelly. He allowed seven shots past him for the night though, sealing the fate of Cleveland's brutal 7-2 loss, the fifth in a six-game losing streak for the Barons.

Bruins right wing Terry O'Reilly closes in on the puck as Barons defenseman Greg Smith and left wing Rick Jodzio (acquired midseason from Colorado) close in on him. The March 21, 1978, matchup ended in a 5-3 loss for Cleveland in one of the final home games for the franchise.

THE NHL BARONS

In this October 1977 game, Barons forward Dennis Maruk evades Kings goalie Rogatien Vachon (the puck is near Vachon's left knee) and defenseman Bob Murdoch to score a goal in the second period. Scoring on Vachon was no easy feat; he won the NHL's coveted Vezina Trophy for best goaltender in the 1967–1968 season. Vachon played a career-high 70 games in the 1977–1978 season, posting a 29-27-13 record. Maruk was the strongest offensive weapon Cleveland had and led the team with 71 points that season. His goal would be a bright spot in an otherwise poor season-long showing versus the Kings. Cleveland won one game against Los Angeles in 1977–1978.

Cleveland center Walt McKechnie and forward Al MacAdam (No. 25) give congratulations to goalie Gilles Meloche, who shut out the Red Wings 2-0 on February 1, 1978. It would be the Barons' only shutout of the season. This was McKechnie's first season in Cleveland since he played for the AHL Barons in the 1970–1971 season. After a 15-year NHL career, McKechnie retired and now runs a family-style restaurant named McKecks in Ontario.

4

HOCKEY RETURNS
TO CLEVELAND

A lot happened in Cleveland sports between the years of 1978 and 1992. Indians pitcher Len Barker tossed a perfect game, Bernie Kosar's Browns fell a game short of the Super Bowl three times in four years, and Michael Jordan hit "The Shot" and destroyed a would-be dream season for the Cavs.

All the while, local hockey fans had no team to call their own. It appeared the city that supported professional hockey for five decades would never get the chance again.

Then, an old friend resurfaced. Larry Gordon, once a marketing professional for Nick Mileti during the days of the Crusaders and current owner of the Muskegon Lumberjacks, submitted a request to move his team to Cleveland. On March 31, 1992, the International Hockey League's board of governors voted unanimously to approve the move. The headline in the following day's Cleveland *Plain Dealer* read, "It's official: Hockey returning to Cleveland."

With intentions of playing in the new downtown arena, the Cleveland Lumberjacks would begin where the NHL Barons left off 14 years ago, in the Richfield Coliseum. While still a great facility for a minor-league team, the Coliseum was not the same place it was in 1978, and the location so far away from downtown Cleveland remained less than ideal.

Nonetheless, a respectable 7,232 fans attended the 'Jacks first home game in Cleveland, a 5-2 win over the Cincinnati Cyclones on October 10, 1992. The night was not without flaws, however. While not as bad as the ice issues that twice canceled the 1974 Crusaders opener, the Coliseum struck again. Late in the second period, a transformer blew, darkening the arena and halting play for 54 grueling minutes. By the time play resumed, it was 11:01 p.m. After the game, Larry Gordon did some damage control as quoted in the Plain Dealer: "In the 18 years the Coliseum has been open, this never happened before," he said. "It was beyond anybody's control. We do want fans to know a game usually doesn't last four hours."

Although the Lumberjacks' first two seasons in Cleveland did not yield as many wins as the organization would have liked, the fans were treated to two of the best offensive players in the history of the IHL in the twilight of their careers. Longtime friends and teammates Jock Callander and Dave Michayluk each had modest NHL experience but were IHL legends.

Michayluk played five seasons in Cleveland before retiring as the IHL's all-time leading goal scorer with 547. Callander remained with the club as a player through the 1999–2000 season and finished as the IHL's all-time leading point scorer and fourth all-time goal scorer.

The Lumberjacks drew well in Richfield, averaging more than 5,200 fans a game the first two years. The move downtown to the sparkling new Gund Arena in 1994, however, would result in a remarkable spike in fan interest. The team topped the 350,000 mark in attendance for the season while averaging 8,542 per contest. The next few seasons saw the 'Jacks shatter Cleveland hockey attendance records as fans flocked to the new arena.

Because the Lumberjacks were a pro hockey team playing in Cleveland, it only made sense they would eventually run into financial troubles. A key blow was losing their affiliation with the Pittsburgh Penguins. Like the Crusaders, the Lumberjacks' fiscal woes were a sign of league-wide trouble. Other IHL teams began losing NHL affiliations to the rival AHL. As teams dropped out of the league, the writing was on the wall.

Attendance dipped drastically to 4,227 in 2000–2001 as Larry Gordon dumped the team on local businessman Hank Kassigkeit. The team nearly folded midseason (sound familiar?), and by the end of the year, it was clear the 'Jacks were not coming back. The entire IHL folded in 2001 with the AHL absorbing just six of the franchises. The Lumberjacks were not one of them.

The city would not have to wait long this time for another on-ice tenant. The very next season, the San Jose Sharks, with George and Gordon Gund as part owners, purchased their AHL affiliate, the Kentucky Thoroughblades, and moved them to Cleveland. In what might be seen as a stark lack of creativity to the outside world, the Thoroughblades were renamed—that's right—the Barons.

The latest edition of the Barons opened on October 5, 2001, just weeks after the September 11 terrorist attacks. Opening night included an emotional tribute to the 9/11 victims as well as Cleveland hockey legend Fred Glover, who had passed away two months prior. The organization also attempted to connect with the past with Barons players from the first era raising a banner to honor the team's nine Calder Cups. The current players hurled top hats into the crowd.

The only thing missing on opening night was the fans. As an ominous sign, just 5,566 attended the inaugural game for the new Barons. It would only get worse from there for an organization that never really connected with the local fan base. To make matters even bleaker, the team did not win. A 29-40-11 first season was followed up by an abysmal 22-48-10 second year. While they qualified for the AHL playoffs in year three, the Barons were easily ousted and returned to mediocrity the next two seasons.

In five seasons, the Barons' average attendance never topped the 4,227 low-water mark the Lumberjacks averaged while desperately trying to stay afloat the previous season. Not surprisingly, the transient franchise packed up and moved again, this time to Massachusetts to become the Worcester Sharks. Cleveland had lost yet another team and the local hockey community desperately needed a shot in the arm—and another team.

When the Muskegon Lumberjacks relocated to Cleveland in 1992, it marked the end of a 14-year pro hockey drought in northeast Ohio. The Lumberjacks started in the Richfield Coliseum and moved to the Gund Arena (now Quicken Loans Arena) in 1994. Seen here is goaltender Zac Bierk, who set a franchise mark by recording six shutouts during the 2000–2001 season. Bierk might best be known as the brother of Sebastian Bach, former lead singer for the band Skid Row. (Larry Hamel-Lambert/ *The Plain Dealer*/Landov.)

Lumberjacks center Brett Bonin takes a shot from Cincinnati Cyclones defenseman Len Esau during a 7-4 Cleveland loss on December 9, 2000. Bonin was the most productive offensive player for the 'Jacks during the 2000-2001 season, scoring 77 points in 72 games. (Steve Cutri/ *The Plain Dealer*/Landov.)

Orlando Solar Bears defenseman Brett Clark gets physical with Cleveland's Brian Bonin during a game at Gund Arena. Clark would go on to enjoy a nice career in the NHL, playing nearly 700 games with four different teams. (Larry Hamel-Lambert/*The Plain Dealer*/Landov.)

The second man to own the Lumberjacks, local businessman Hank Kassigkeit (right) speaks with legendary hall-of-famer Gordie Howe prior to a game at Gund Arena. Kassigkeit was known for his friendly, hands-on approach with the fans; however, the team was in dire financial straits when he took control. Ultimately, there was little Kassigkeit could do as the team folded along with the entire league in 2001. Although some IHL teams were absorbed into the American Hockey League, the Lumberjacks were not one of the lucky ones selected. (Larry Hamel-Lambert/*The Plain Dealer*/Landov.)

Brian Bonin makes a tremendous play to score on Cincinnati Cyclones netminder Corey Hirsch while getting pushed from behind by Cyclone defender Harlan Pratt. Goals did not come easy that year on Hirsch, who was 11-2 with a 2.15 goals against average and boasted a save percentage of .935. While Bonin was a very good minor professional hockey player, he never registered a point in 12 National Hockey League games with the Pittsburgh Penguins and Minnesota Wild. (Steve Cutri/*The Plain Dealer*/Landov.)

Cleveland players celebrate a 3-2 shootout win over the Orlando Solar Bears on November 25, 2000. Although they never brought a Turner Cup to northeast Ohio, the Lumberjacks were mostly successful during their nine seasons. They qualified for the International Hockey League playoffs in all but two of them. (Larry Hamel-Lambert/ *The Plain Dealer*/Landov.)

Orlando defenseman Hugo Boisvert, who played at Ohio State University, attempts to block a pass from Lumberjacks defenseman Nick Naumenko. They did not enjoy good fan support during their six seasons in the IHL, but the Orlando Solar Bears were successful on the ice, winning the league's final Turner Cup in 2001. (Larry Hamel-Lambert/*The Plain Dealer*/Landov.)

Lumberjack center Brett McLean (right) slides around Grand Rapids Griffins defender Petr Schastlivy during an October 2000 game. McLean caught on as a full-time NHL player with the Chicago Blackhawks, Colorado Avalanche, and Florida Panthers after leaving Cleveland. In 2009, he moved overseas to play in the Swiss professional league. (Scott Shaw/ *The Plain Dealer*/Landov.)

Cleveland's left wing Pat Rissmiller (No. 26) prepares to pass the puck as Manitoba defenseman Prestin Ryan (No. 6) and right wing Jason King (No. 32) close in on him. The Barons would lose five of eight matchups in the 2005–2006 season against the Moose. Rissmiller would be called up to the San Jose Sharks the same season. (Courtesy Jay Sharp.)

Cleveland goalie Zac Bierk (No. 30) battles Grand Rapids' Chris Szysky for puck possession behind the net during a game in Michigan. The Griffins, known for filling their arena, finished 53-22-7 in 2000–2001 and were quickly accepted into the American Hockey League in 2001. (TJ Hamilton/ *The Plain Dealer*/Landov.)

Cleveland's Brett McLean eludes Grand Rapids defender Sean Gagnon on April 25, 2001, during the Griffins' 3-0 victory. With the win, Grand Rapids eliminated the Lumberjacks from the playoffs in what would be the final game in team history. (Mike Levy/*The Plain Dealer*/Landov.)

Barons center Craig Valette (No. 12) watches as the pucks sails wide of the net. Manitoba goalie Wade Flaherty (No. 33), and defenseman James DeMone prepare to defend against oncoming Cleveland skaters. Flaherty, a veteran NHL goalie, came down to the AHL in the 2002–2003 season and would finish out his career there in 2007–2008. (Courtesy Jay Sharp.)

Cleveland Barons six-foot, two-inch right wing Tim Conboy (No. 4), known for his role as an enforcer and his physical playing style, takes control of the puck in a game against the Manitoba Moose. Conboy was brought to Cleveland to help with a playoff run in the 2003–2004 season. (Courtesy Jay Sharp.)

Cleveland Barons defenseman Ray DiLauro fights for possession of the puck with an unseen Manitoba skater. DiLauro played one season with the Barons but is most notable for scoring a hat trick in only 40 seconds while playing for the Reading Royals in the East Coast Hockey League's 2002–2003 season. (Courtesy Jay Sharp.)

Barons defenseman Garrett Stafford (No. 8) battles Manitoba defenseman Sven Butenschoen (No. 52) for control of the puck as the teams clash in front of a sparse crowd at the Quicken Loans Arena (formerly Gund Arena). Butenschoen had once called Cleveland home as a member of the Lumberjacks during the IHL team's 1996–1997 season. (Courtesy Jay Sharp.)

Cleveland goalie Nolan Schaefer (No. 27) eyes the action down ice as he stands in goal during this November 2005 matchup with Manitoba. Schaefer would go on to win the Harry "Hap" Holmes Award for lowest goals against average with the Houston Aeros in 2007–2008. (Courtesy Jay Sharp.)

It's sticks to the sky as Cleveland Barons players hit the ice to celebrate following their 3-2 win against the Manitoba Moose on November 12, 2005, in front of a crowd of just over 4,000 fans. Visible are forwards Steve Bernier (No. 16), Tim Conboy (No. 4), Craig Valette (No. 12), and Brad Staubitz (No. 3). (Courtesy Jay Sharp.)

Cleveland defenseman Aaron Power (No. 57) fires a pass down ice as the action heats up during this contest with the Manitoba Moose. Barons center Tom Cavanagh (No. 20) watches the action as he skates in. With so few filled seats in the house, the faithful fans needed something to cheer about. (Courtesy Jay Sharp.)

Garrett Stafford (No. 8), a defenseman for Cleveland, withstands a collision with a Manitoba Moose player and maintains control of the puck as his teammates race down ice. Stafford set the team record for most points by a defenseman in the 2003–2004 season with 46 points scored. (Courtesy Jay Sharp.)

5

CLEVELAND HOCKEY'S
FIRST FAMILY

It would be easy to drive right past Jim Fritsche's hockey shop and skills center on Ridge Road in Parma and not even realize it. Inside, one will find a gruff yet friendly man who just so happens to be the patriarch of Cleveland's most accomplished hockey family.

Jim Fritsche put two sons into professional hockey while raising them in a football-crazed town. His oldest son, Dan, played in 256 NHL games over five seasons for the Columbus Blue Jackets, New York Rangers, and Minnesota Wild. His younger son Tom went from the US National Development Team to the Ohio State University squad on a scholarship before playing three seasons with the Lake Erie Monsters.

While other kids may have wanted to become the next Bernie Kosar or Jim Thome, the Fritsche brothers were proficient skaters by their fifth birthday. Before long, they were playing for the Parma Flyers youth team as well as practicing relentlessly at the game they loved.

As the brothers got older, they began playing for the elite Cleveland Barons AAA youth teams. For Jim Fritsche, this would require an extraordinary commitment for his sons to fully reach their potential. Weekends were spent traveling out of state to places like Michigan and Illinois to play greater competition. It was a tall order for a man running a business and raising two younger daughters as well.

"We were fortunate to have a father who pushed us and did all the little things to help us get to where we ended up," Dan said. "I don't know how he did it with four children and a business."

"Our dad used to use his own money to rent ice time at Forestwood (now Michael A. Ries) ice rink so we could practice every day," Tom added.

The time and effort paid off as the hockey world began to take notice of the Fritsche boys.

"At 15 years old, I was getting approached by agents, teams and colleges," Dan said. "That's when it clicked that this dream can become a reality."

"When they were about 13, I thought they could both go on to play collegiately," Jim said. "Tom was a late bloomer, he really came on about age 14, but Danny was real good at 12."

When he was 16 years old, Dan was drafted by the Sarnia Sting of the Ontario Hockey League. In hockey, major junior leagues are known to be the fast track to the NHL. Not long after, Tom was selected to play for the US National Development Team in Ann Arbor, Michigan.

Suddenly, Jim Fritsche's house appeared much more spacious. With one son in Sarnia, Ontario, and another in Michigan, his life seemingly became a constant road trip. Jim's willingness to travel helped both boys, who were each dealing with homesickness.

"The first year away I would take the three and a half hour drive home every time we had a day and a half off," Dan said. "I never thought I would miss home so much. I don't think my dad missed a game all year, which made things a lot easier on me. I look back on that and hope one day I can make the same commitment to my kids."

Rather than play major junior hockey like his brother, Tom opted to play for the Ohio State Buckeyes after two years on the development team. Understanding it would delay his path to professional hockey, Tom chose college hockey to make himself a more complete player.

"I went to college because I wasn't as highly touted as Dan," he said. "Going to college makes it longer to get to the pros, but you are usually a more developed player."

In a remarkable twist of fate, Dan was unexpectedly selected by the Columbus Blue Jackets with the 46th overall pick in the 2003 NHL draft. Though he had not counted them as one of his potential suitors, Dan was thrilled to be a member of the Blue Jackets, which afforded him a chance to play early for a young organization. Also, it was less than two hours from home.

With Dan being drafted by the Blue Jackets and Tom going to Ohio State, the brothers moved into a Columbus condominium together, along with a couple of their childhood buddies. It was an experience Dan describes as the best time of his life.

"He loved it because he acted like he went to Ohio State," Tom recalled laughing. "He loves OSU more than I do and I went there."

Tom was selected 47th overall by the Colorado Avalanche. He would finish his four-year career with Ohio State before formally signing with the Avalanche. Late in his college years he attended a Colorado development camp where he found out he would be starting his pro career in Cleveland with Colorado's American Hockey League affiliate, the Lake Erie Monsters.

"I loved it," he said. "Cleveland is the nicest place to go in the AHL and Quicken Loans Arena is unbelievable compared to other arenas in the league. Plus, I left home at 15 years old; I didn't need to go anywhere else."

Back in Columbus, Dan was settling in nicely with the Blue Jackets. Carrying the momentum from the gold medal performance in Helsinki, he scored two goals in Washington, D.C. against the Capitals in the first game of the 2005–2006 season.

Dan would enjoy other big moments with the Blue Jackets. There was another two-goal performance versus the Ottawa Senators in December 2006. He scored a goal in four straight games from January 19 to 30, 2007. Unfortunately, Columbus traded him to the New York Rangers in 2008. Dan's time with the Rangers was brief and he was dealt to the Minnesota Wild the same season.

In Cleveland, Tom joined the Monsters during the second half of the team's inaugural season. Like a Hollywood script, he scored his first professional goal in his first game in Cleveland on March 18, 2008, versus the Chicago Wolves. His performance that night earned him the game's First Star.

Tom would go on to play three seasons with the Monsters before health problems cut his promising career short. Still, he enjoyed some great moments playing in his hometown. He recalls Parma hockey kids coming to the games to see one of their own playing. When the Monsters would make players available after games for fan autographs, Tom's teammates would give him a hard time because so many fans wanted to talk to him about people they knew, or experiences they had with his father.

As for Jim Fritsche, he continues to run his skill center in Parma, teaching hockey to kids from age 7 to 15, and he remains proud of all his kids. One cannot tell the story of Cleveland hockey without mentioning the name "Fritsche"—the first family of Cleveland hockey.

Brothers Tom (left) and Dan Fritsche took different paths and ended up in Columbus together. Tom went to The Ohio State University on an athletic scholarship while Dan was drafted by the NHL's Columbus Blue Jackets. The brothers lived together in a condominium in Columbus with childhood friends from the Cleveland area. Dan was able to experience a taste of the college life, something he bypassed in favor of major junior hockey in Canada. Likewise, Tom was able to catch a glimpse of the day-to-day life of a professional hockey player, a life he would live a few years down the road. (Courtesy of Fritsche family.)

Here is a look at where it all started. Like thousands of other northeast Ohio kids, the Fritsche brothers started playing with the Parma Flyers youth hockey program. The Flyers have been run by the Parma Hockey Association since 1971. Dan joined Brian Holzinger and Mike Rupp as the third former Flyer to play in the NHL. (Courtesy of Fritsche family)

Dan played for the Sarnia Sting of the Ontario Hockey League, opting to play in Canada rather than college. Major junior hockey leagues are known to be a fast track to the professional level for players who possess that level of talent. (Courtesy of Fritsche family.)

Tom played for the hometown Lake Erie Monsters. Having already traveled a great deal for hockey, he welcomed the opportunity to come home and play in front of family and friends. Tom scored his first career professional goal in his first home game against the Chicago Wolves. (Courtesy of Fritsche family.)

#49 Dan Fritsche

He played for three NHL teams, but Dan performed best during his time with the Blue Jackets, scoring 29 of his 34 career goals. Columbus selected him in the second round with the 46th overall pick in the 2003 NHL entry draft. He played his first NHL game at just 18 years old. (Courtesy of Fritsche family.)

"When I was a kid, some of my friends didn't even know what hockey was," Dan recalled. "They didn't understand the concept of me playing hockey, but for my brother and I that is all life was. Before we could walk we were skating because it is what we loved." Jim Fritsche often rented ice time with his own money so the brothers could work on things that he noticed needed improvement from previous games. (Courtesy of Fritsche family.)

"Putting on an NHL sweater for the first time was the realization of my childhood dreams," Dan explained. "My first game I just wanted to play with high energy, safe and make a lot of hits. As time went on, nerves went down, confidence went up and I kind of grew into a nice role with the Columbus organization. It was a good time for me." Jim Fritsche recalls going to Columbus every weekend to watch his sons play. It was a lot of miles logged but also memories he would not trade for anything. (Courtesy of Fritsche family.)

6

Monsters to the North!

Local hockey fans began to feel like Cleveland was professional hockey's bus station: teams just stopped briefly on their way to somewhere else. The apathetic response to the last Barons team led many to wonder if the city could even support professional hockey anymore.

Dan Gilbert did not agree with that sentiment. Just weeks after the Barons played their final game in Cleveland, Gilbert purchased the dormant Utah Grizzlies American Hockey League franchise with intentions of moving them to Cleveland. Gilbert was the ideal man to stabilize the local hockey scene. He was already wildly successful, a founder and chairman of Quicken Loans Inc., when he purchased the Cleveland Cavaliers in 2005.

Although the Cavaliers already had superstar LeBron James on the roster, Gilbert overhauled the organization. Within two years, the Cavaliers made their first NBA finals appearance after nearly 40 years of frustration. Unlike other sports team owners in town, Gilbert had a reputation for freely spending money to produce results. It was extremely appealing to the average Cleveland sports fan.

Gilbert's team did everything different than previous franchises. Rather than trot out a team name and uniform theme from the past, the new team was dubbed the "Lake Erie Monsters." To go with the catchy name, the Monsters also featured sharp, fresh uniforms with a recognizable logo. As a minor-league team, the Monsters would be at the mercy of their parent club as to how much talent was on the ice, but the Gilbert ownership made sure every other aspect of the game was a top-notch experience for the fans.

It was evident on opening night the Lake Erie marketing machine knew what it was doing. A huge crowd of 15,132 crammed through the turnstiles to welcome the new squad on October 6, 2007. Although the initial season was disappointing in the league standings, fans continued to support the team, as Lake Erie was 11th out of the 29 AHL teams in attendance.

As the team improved, fans continued to be drawn towards the party-like atmosphere at Monsters games. Despite narrowly missing the playoffs the next two seasons, the Monsters jumped to ninth and sixth in league attendance in 2008–2009 and 2009–2010 respectively.

The 2010–2011 season brought a nice mix of capable veterans and developing youngsters. Lake Erie also enjoyed one of the best goalie tandems in the AHL in 35-year-old NHL veteran John Grahame and returning Monsters 27-year-old Jason Bacashihua. With the team hovering around the .500 mark, they suddenly hit their stride sparked by a five-game winning streak in early February. Bacashihua won four of the games, surrendering just six goals.

On March 11, the Monsters embarked on a five-game road trip to be played in nine days. Shockingly, Lake Erie won all five, then after a home victory, won two more road games in Rochester and Toronto for an improbable eight-game winning streak that included seven road victories. Cleveland had the hottest team in the AHL and had finally secured a spot in the Calder Cup playoffs.

The Monsters were matched with a tough Manitoba Moose team in the first-round playoff series. Arena personnel passed out playoff-themed t-shirts and white towels as fans entered the gates. The faithful were ready. By the opening faceoff, a sea of waving towels could be seen in the stands.

After four games, Lake Erie appeared as the superior team, grabbing a 3-1 series lead. The Moose replaced goalie Tyler Weiman, a popular former Monster, with Eddie Lack. The much taller Lack was simply impenetrable for the remainder of the series. Even though the Monsters outshot Manitoba 88-69 the final three games of the series, Lack allowed just two goals in a performance for the ages. More than 10,000 fans left Quicken Loans Arena heartbroken as the Moose escaped with a game-seven win to take the series.

By averaging 8,069 spectators for their four playoff games, the Monsters led the AHL in playoff attendance in 2011. After the season, the organization was recognized by the league with the Outstanding Fan Experience Award. While the Monsters were eliminated from playoff contention on the final game of the next season, they jumped to third in attendance in the now 30-team league with 7,845 arriving for each tilt. It was evident the latest hockey team to represent the city of Cleveland was here to stay.

It has been nearly a century since the first professional hockey team took to the ice in Cleveland. The Lake Erie Monsters are the latest in a long line of teams that have played in various leagues and arenas over the years. Each of the teams has enjoyed differing levels of popularity, but no team since the original AHL Barons has existed for a full decade. With Dan Gilbert's Monsters and the AHL, Cleveland has a stability not seen in a long time in the northeast Ohio hockey scene. Local fans responded to this team, even before the Monsters seriously contended for a championship.

The professional hockey history of Cleveland is quite a roller-coaster ride, from the glory days of the old Barons in the Cleveland Arena to the financial struggles of the teams in the 1970s. It is difficult for minor league franchises to compete in cities with major-league teams. Cleveland blew its chance at major-league hockey when the NHL Barons dissolved, although one can debate for hours whether the city was actually given a fair chance to succeed. When the Columbus Blue Jackets began play in the NHL, it closed the books on Cleveland ever returning to the big leagues.

The Lake Erie Monsters are proving minor-league hockey can flourish while competing with the big boys. Northeast Ohio is so starved for a sports championship, the Monsters could conceivably own the town if they were to make a serious run at a Calder Cup, let alone win one. Only time will tell when and how this latest chapter ends. But if history teaches anything, it is to just enjoy the ride and keep your eyes on the puck.

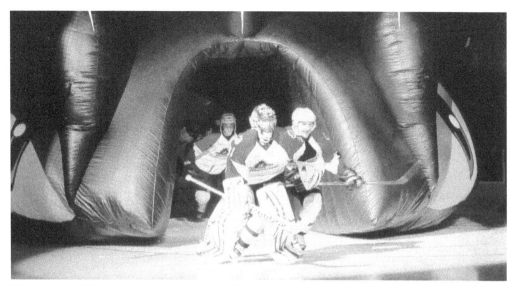

Skating out of their signature "monster head," the Lake Erie Monsters took the ice in 2007 to start the latest chapter of professional hockey history in Cleveland. The Monsters were born when the defunct Utah Grizzlies of the AHL were purchased by Cleveland Cavaliers owner Dan Gilbert on May 16, 2006. Gilbert believed hockey could be successful in Cleveland with the right approach. Chosen to represent the Lake Erie region, rather than just Cleveland proper, the Monsters are the top affiliate of the NHL's Colorado Avalanche. The first game brought 15,132 fans through the gates and the team has enjoyed good support since. With a unique and dynamic marketing strategy, the Monsters are built to last in Cleveland, as they hope to become the first team since 1973 to survive for more than a decade in northeast Ohio. (Courtesy of the Lake Erie Monsters.)

Goalie Tyler Weiman was wildly popular during his time in Cleveland, even getting his own bobblehead promotion in 2010. Weiman recorded 13 shutouts playing parts of three seasons with the Monsters and appeared in an AHL all-star same. (Courtesy Melissa Hess/Hossenfeffer Photo.)

Fire shoots out of the scoreboard during pregame player introductions prior to a Monsters game against the Texas Stars in January 2010. It is another example of how games are now presented as a total entertainment experience to appeal to a larger demographic. This particular night, the Monsters packed more than 18,000 fans into the Quicken Loans Arena. (Courtesy of the Lake Erie Monsters.)

A routine custom before Lake Erie games, a youth hockey team lines up alongside the Monsters' starting line for the singing of "The Star-Spangled Banner." Since their inception, the Monsters players and professional staff have been active in the community. The American Hockey League recognized the organization in 2010 with the annual award for exceptional community service. (Courtesy of the Lake Erie Monsters.)

While not easy to compete as a minor-league team in a city with three major-league franchises, the Monsters have enjoyed consistently good fan support since arriving in Cleveland. The team has ranked in the top ten in the American Hockey League in attendance every season except the first when they were 11th. Since the original AHL Cleveland Barons moved to Jacksonville, Florida, and folded, no professional hockey team in Cleveland has celebrated a decade of existence. (Courtesy of the Lake Erie Monsters.)

Right wing Dan Dasilva sets a screen on the Philadelphia Phantoms goaltender during a 2008 game. The Monsters eventually dropped the "M" from the front of their sweaters and replaced it with the team's official logo. A popular black alternate jersey was also added. (Courtesy Melissa Hess/Hossenfeffer Photo.)

The Monsters locker room in Quicken Loans Arena sits vacant in preparation for the players' arrival for a game. The white jerseys seen here are the team's primary home uniforms with a popular black alternate jersey being the secondary option. The recognizable logo was designed for the team to create its own identity rather than piggyback on a team from years past. (Courtesy of the Lake Erie Monsters.)

Left wing Matt Ford and center Julian Talbot celebrate a goal during a 2010 game. The duo would play for two very different "Bears" teams the next season. Ford moved on to the Hershey Bears, while Talbot signed with the Berlin Polar Bears of the German Hockey League. (Courtesy of the Lake Erie Monsters.)

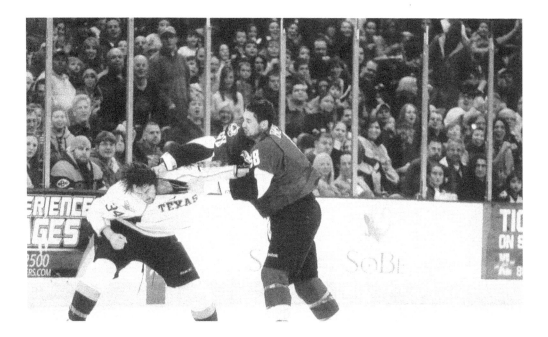

One of the most popular players to wear a Monsters uniform was big forward Patrick Bordeleau. Seen here in his most familiar pose, he is fighting with Luke Gadzic of the Texas Stars. Bordeleau was the epitome of an enforcer for Lake Erie, preventing opposing players from taking liberties with his teammates. Using his six-foot-six-inch frame and long reach to his advantage, Bordeleau quickly earned a reputation as someone to avoid mixing it up with. The Montreal native unofficially compiled a 35-6-6 fight record in the AHL. (Both, courtesy of the Lake Erie Monsters.)

Cleveland sports fans—starved for a winner—came out in droves and proudly waved their "playoff hankies" when the Monsters qualified for the Calder Cup playoffs in 2011. Lake Erie led the league in playoff attendance with 8,069 crossing the turnstiles per contest. There were 10,277 on hand to witness the Monsters' heartbreaking game-seven, series-deciding defeat to the Manitoba Moose. (Courtesy of the Lake Erie Monsters.)

Pictured is a pause in action during the seventh and deciding game of a Calder Cup playoff series with the Manitoba Moose. Despite building a 3-1 series lead after four games, the Monsters dropped the final three games of the series when Manitoba goaltender Eddie Lack caught fire. Lack allowed just two Lake Erie goals over three games to slam the door on the Monsters' promising season. (Courtesy of the Lake Erie Monsters.)

Monsters seagull mascot Sullivan C. Goal or "Sully" is among the most popular mascots in town, performing acrobatic tricks in the stands and skating on the ice. (Courtesy of the Lake Erie Monsters.)

Among the popular promotions each year are specialty jerseys designed to coincide with the theme of the night, which are often auctioned off to fans after the game. Here, Monsters players Luke Walker (left) and Justin Mercier celebrate a goal wearing Cleveland Browns themed jerseys on the night they honored the National Football League team. (Courtesy of the Lake Erie Monsters.)

Standing at center ice on Cleveland Browns appreciation night are Browns players (from left to right) cornerback Joe Haden, Monsters mascot Sully, safety T.J. Ward, Monsters in-game host Olivier Sedra, wide receiver Jordan Norwood, and wide receiver/kick returner Josh Cribbs. Also in attendance were several Browns alumni who made themselves available to mingle with the crowd. (Courtesy of the Lake Erie Monsters.)

Cleveland Cavaliers star rookies Tristan Thompson (No. 13) and Kyrie Irving (No. 2) meet at center ice for the ceremonial puck drop with a local Boy Scout during a 2011–2012 season game. The Monsters enjoy a good working relationship with the other professional sports teams in town. Taking the faceoff are Monsters captain David Liffiton (left) and Colin Stuart of the Rochester Americans. (Courtesy of the Lake Erie Monsters.)

A giant crowd of 18,626 was on hand to watch the Monsters defeat the Texas Stars 5-4 in overtime on January 22, 2010. The game was dubbed "Shaq Bobblehead Night" and featured a bobblehead figure of Cleveland Cavalier and NBA legend Shaquille O'Neal dressed like a Lake Erie hockey player. (Courtesy of the Lake Erie Monsters.)

The Monsters' first line is prepared for battle: from left to right are left wing Justin Mercier, right wing Matt Ford, defensemen Shawn Belle and Steve Oleksy, and center Julian Talbot prior to a 2011 matchup. Belle was acquired by the Colorado Avalanche from the Edmonton Oilers to assist the Monsters with a playoff run. (Courtesy of the Lake Erie Monsters.)

Monsters Dean Strong (left) and David Van Der Gulik prepare for a faceoff while wearing green and white shamrock-themed uniforms in honor of St. Patrick's Day 2012. The Monsters lost to the Chicago Wolves 1-0 despite an outstanding effort from goaltender Cedric Desjardins, who turned away 41 of 42 shots. (Courtesy of the Lake Erie Monsters.)

Goalie Jason Bacashihua plays the puck behind the net. The Dearborn Heights, Michigan, native played two stints with the Monsters, playing exceptionally well during the 2010–2011 season. That year "Cash" went 23-16-3 with a 2.29 goals against average. Bacashihua ironically began his American Hockey League career with the Utah Grizzlies, who later became the Monsters. (Courtesy of the Lake Erie Monsters.)

The Monsters are in action during the annual "Pink the Rink" game in 2011. Beginning in 2009, the Monsters started playing one game each year with the ice painted pink and pink-themed uniforms to raise donations and awareness for breast cancer. The first attempt in 2009 resulted in a game postponement when the pink dye started to melt the ice and made skating virtually impossible. (Both, courtesy of the Lake Erie Monsters.)

Defenseman Wes O'Neill was a solid blue-line contributor for the Monsters during the team's first three seasons. Here he is seen delivering a shot to Hershey Bears center Jason Morgan. O'Neill played brief stints with the Colorado Avalanche. (Courtesy Melissa Hess/Hossenfeffer Photo.)

Originally drafted by the Columbus Blue Jackets in the 2003 NHL entry draft, center Phillippe Dupuis was a big source of offensive production for the Monsters from 2007 to 2010. Dupuis made the 2010–2011 Colorado Avalanche roster and played 74 games for the big club. (Courtesy Melissa Hess/Hossenfeffer Photo.)

Shown is the interior of the Quicken Loans Arena, which was originally the Gund Arena. "The Q" was built as part of the Gateway Project, which placed a new arena and baseball-only stadium side-by-side in the heart of downtown Cleveland. The opening of the arena meant the return of hockey to downtown for the first time in 20 years. (Courtesy of the Lake Erie Monsters.)

Like the Richfield Coliseum, the Quicken Loans Arena has housed three professional hockey teams. The Cleveland Lumberjacks were popular but folded in 2001 along with the International Hockey League. The third edition of the Barons never connected with locals and moved to Worcester, Massachusetts, in 2006. The arena is the current home of the Lake Erie Monsters of the American Hockey League. (Courtesy of the Lake Erie Monsters.)

Visit us at
arcadiapublishing.com

CPSIA information can be obtained
at www.ICGtesting.com
Printed in the USA
LVHW022153231219
641492LV00014B/138/P